16.95

THE BORDER WORKBOOK

Easy Speed-Pieced & *Foundation-Pieced Borders*

JANET KIME

That Patchwork Place®

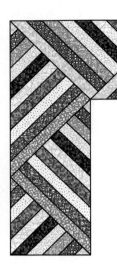

Credits

Editor-in-Chief	Kerry I. Smith
Technical Editor	Laura M. Reinstatler
Managing Editor	Judy Petry
Design Director	Cheryl Stevenson
Text and Cover Designer	Amy Shayne
Design Assistant	Marijane E. Figg
Copy Editor	Liz McGehee
Proofreader	Kathleen Pike
Illustrator	Robin Strobel
Photographer	Brent Kane

MISSION STATEMENT

WE ARE DEDICATED TO PROVIDING
QUALITY PRODUCTS AND SERVICE BY
WORKING TOGETHER TO INSPIRE CREATIVITY
AND TO ENRICH THE LIVES WE TOUCH.

The Border Workbook: Easy Speed-Pieced and
Foundation-Pieced Borders
© 1997 by Janet Kime
That Patchwork Place, Inc., PO Box 118, Bothell, WA
98041-0118 USA

Printed in the United States of America
02 01 00 99 98   6 5 4 3

The information in this book is presented in good faith, but no warranty is given nor results guaranteed. Since That Patchwork Place, Inc., has no control over choice of materials or procedures, the company assumes no responsibility for the use of this information.

Library of Congress Cataloging-in-Publication Data

Kime, Janet,
    The border workbook : easy speed-pieced and foundation-pieced borders / Janet Kime.
        p.   cm.
    ISBN 1-56477-184-9
    1. Patchwork quilts. 2. Borders, Ornamental (Decorative arts)
I. Title.
TT835.K49495   1997   97-3682
746.46—dc21   CIP

TABLE OF CONTENTS

INTRODUCTION

For years, I have taught border classes in which students practice speed-piecing techniques and develop an arsenal of eight or nine border designs. Based on the comments of my students and the quilt tops they bring to class, it appears many quilters find themselves with a quilt top they think needs a border. But either they don't know which border, they don't have much fabric left, or they don't want to spend much more time on the quilt top.

If you have found yourself in a similar situation, this book is for you. Presented here are twenty-seven different border designs, most including directions for several sizes. Your fabric selection can dramatically change the appearance of the borders; the illustrations suggest some of the possibilities. With all the sizes and variations, you can prepare hundreds of different borders.

None of the borders requires templates. Most are speed-pieced and go together quickly. Some are foundation-pieced versions that take more time to assemble, but these borders are scaled for small or miniature quilts, so you don't need yards and yards of border. To help you choose a border for a miniature quilt, the foundation-piecing patterns are grouped together on pages 90–94.

Sample yardages are included so you can estimate how much additional fabric to buy for your border—or, if you are adding a border to a completed top, whether you have enough fabric left. And don't panic—the chapter "Planning Your Border" on pages 5–12 includes suggestions for substituting fabrics if you don't have enough left over from the quilt top.

With this book as your guide, you should be able to find and sew the perfect border for your quilt.

PLANNING YOUR BORDER

Selecting a Design

How do you decide whether your quilt needs a border? How do you decide which border design is best?

The answer to the first question is this: Your quilt needs a border if you think it needs one. There aren't any rules. If your quilt top looks finished to you without a border, it is. But if it looks like it needs something around the edges, or if you need it to be bigger, then add a border.

The simplest borders are plain strips of fabric, sometimes one wide strip, sometimes several strips of varying widths. These are the borders we all are comfortable with, and they are all that many quilts need. Eventually, however, you'll want to experiment with pieced borders. The borders in this book are great ones to start with; they all go together quickly, and cutting measurements are provided for several sizes. But which one is right for your quilt?

To help you choose, all the borders in this book are illustrated along the right edge of the right-hand pages so you can flip through the book quickly and see all the borders. Make a sketch of a section of your quilt on graph paper. Place the quilt designs next to your favorite borders to have an idea of how the border looks with your quilt top. If you would like to see the effect of changing a border's size, photocopy the border, either enlarging or reducing it.

Although there are no rules about which border goes with which quilt—remember, the border you like is the right border—there are guidelines.

✂ A border design will look more coordinated if it includes some of the same shapes that are in the quilt design. For example, "Sawtooth" borders (page 42) almost always look good on quilts that have half-square triangles in the blocks; "Stacked Strips" (page 46) is a good border for Log Cabin quilts.

✂ If you like a border design, but want something bolder or quieter, try changing the scale. Your choice of fabric can also enliven or tame a border (see "Selecting Fabric" below).

✂ Consider the fabrics you plan to use. The more complicated the border design, the more contrast is necessary between the design and background fabrics. For example, if you are committed to yellow and white, the "Twined Border" (page 79) probably won't work (see "Selecting Fabric" below).

✂ Think about combining two or more pieced borders or repeating the same border in different sizes. For example, you could put a small Zigzag border inside a big, bold Zigzag border.

Selecting Fabric

The fabrics in your border should be the same as those used in the body of the quilt. This is not a hard-and-fast rule, but if you don't use at least some of the same fabrics, the border will look as if it were tacked on as an afterthought. (This may be the case, but it doesn't have to look like it.)

The instructions for each border provide yardage guidelines for bordering a 30" x 45" wall quilt and a 90" x 110" bed quilt. These guidelines will help you estimate how much fabric you'll need for your border. If the body of your quilt has a restricted palette and you don't have much fabric left (and you don't want to add new fabrics), you may have to select a border based on how much fabric it requires.

If you choose a border that requires additional fabric (and, of course, the store no longer has the fabric you need), it is usually better to add a fabric that is similar to your original fabric rather than a fabric that is closer but a near miss. For example, if you can't exactly match the red solid in the quilt, a nearly matching red solid will look exactly like what it is: an unsatisfactory substitute. Forever after, it will

remind you that you ran out of fabric. A better choice might be a subtle red-on-red print that coordinates with your original red; no one would expect it to be an exact match.

Some quilters say you shouldn't use a fabric in your border that isn't in the body of the quilt; but this is your quilt, not theirs. If it looks good to you, there is no reason not to add one or more new fabrics in the border. If there are a number of fabrics in the quilt, additions may not even be noticeable. Look for similar colors in different prints. Or, if your quilt is all prints, consider adding a matching solid to the border. Look also for prints that combine two or three of the colors in your quilt.

If you are really having trouble adding fabrics, consider overdyeing some fabrics to alter the shade of a fabric that isn't quite right. If you feel particularly daring, you can add the border first and then overdye the whole quilt. This process mellows all the colors in one direction, toward brown, gray, or pink, for example, and can coordinate even mismatched fabrics.

Not all fabric combinations can be used successfully in pieced borders. When planning your border, consider the same factors as when planning the body of the quilt: color, scale, and the number of different fabrics to be used.

Color: For a bold border, use solids with a lot of contrast between the dark and light fabrics; for example, solid red and solid white. For a calmer border, use fabrics with less contrast; for example, medium pink and light pink. Colors next to each other on the color wheel, such as blue and lavender, also make a quieter border than colors that are a distance from each other, such as blue and red.

In general, the more complicated the design, the more contrast is needed between the design and background fabrics. The two lines of the "Twined Border" (page 79), for example, are visible only if the fabrics used are distinct from each other and from the background.

Scale: Prints soften the edges of the design, especially if you combine two prints that include some of the same colors. Avoid using two fabrics with the same background color, such as a black background print and black solid. With large-scale prints, you may lose the edges completely.

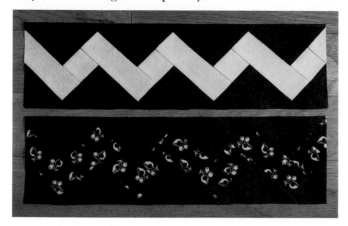

Avoid widely spaced print motifs with the same ground color as the background fabric. The Zigzag design on the top is bold and distinct, but the edges of the Zigzag on the bottom are lost.

Large-scale prints can be effective, as long as the fabric contrasts well with the background fabric. When a large-scale print is broken up into small isolated pieces in a border, the border will look as if it were made from a number of fabrics instead of one speedy strip unit.

This Squares on Point border, made from one large-scale print, looks interestingly scrappy.

Number of fabrics: For a scrappy look, use several different fabrics in the border. For an even scrappier look, use several fabrics for the border design and several for the border background. The chart on page 12 indicates which of the borders in this book are especially good for using small scraps of fabric.

Strip-pieced borders are quick to make if you use one fabric for the border design and one fabric for the border background. If you want to make a scrappy strip-pieced border, make each strip-pieced unit from a different combination of fabrics, then mix the crosscuts as you sew the borders together. (See "Speed Piecing" on page 25.) For a small quilt, make many 10"- to 20"-long strip-pieced units in-stead of a few 44"-long strip-pieced units. This way, you can include more fabrics.

Making a Border That Fits

Piecing a border is only part of the task; the real trick is making it fit your quilt. You can do it, though, even if you think you are a dunce at math. Once you have armed yourself with this book, a tape measure, and your trusty calculator, just follow the steps.

1. Measure the length and the width of your quilt top across the center (not along the edges, which may be distorted). Subtract ½" from each measurement (for seam allowances) to get the fin-ished length and width of the quilt. *Unless otherwise stated, quilt measurements in this book are finished measurements.*

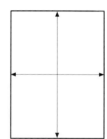

2. Determine the number of border-design repeats you'll need for each border. Round any partial units up for a whole number of repeats.

You want your borders to look like this...

not this.

3. Multiply the number of whole repeats by the length of the repeat unit to determine the actual finished length of each pieced border.

4. Determine the width of the "coping strips" needed to bring your quilt top up to the size of the borders. (Coping strips are the strips added to the quilt top before the pieced border is added.) For example, let's say you have a small quilt, 12" x 15" finished, and you want to add a Squares on Point border with 1" squares. The repeat unit (the length of border occupied by each of the squares) is not 1". Because the squares are turned on point, the repeat unit is the diagonal of the square: 1.41".

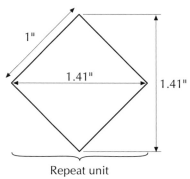

Repeat unit

The closest you can come to the size of your quilt with whole squares is 9 squares in the top and bottom borders (9 x 1.41" = 12.69") and 11 squares in the side borders (11 x 1.41" = 15.51").

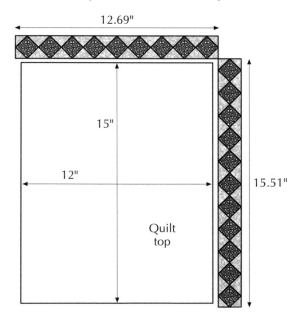

Before you can add your pieced border, you need to add an inner border to make the finished size of your quilt approximately 12.69" x 15.51". In this case, you would add a ⅜"-wide coping strip (plus ½" for seam allowances) to each side edge of the quilt top, and ¼"-wide strips (plus seam allowances) to the top and bottom edges. This would bring the finished size of your quilt top up to 12.75" (or 12¾") x 15.5" (or 15½"), close enough to ease in any differences.

Coping strips

"Wait a minute!" I can hear you quaver. "1.41"? 12.69"? Why can't I plan the border in quarter inches like I'm used to?"

Well, sometimes you can. Some borders do have 2" or 3½" repeats, measurements you are more accustomed to working with. But many of the speed-pieced borders in this book don't. The strip-pieced unit and the crosscut measurements are always listed in quarter inches so you can rotary cut them easily, but at some point in the construction of the border, everything is turned on point. Like the Squares on Point border, you are suddenly dealing with diagonal measurements rather than the measurements of the individual sides of the units.

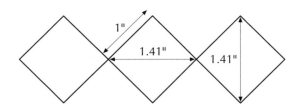

How did I come up with 1.41"? It's actually simple to calculate. Almost all the borders in this book include a half-square triangle, a triangle made by cutting a square in half diagonally. In all such triangles, the length of the long side is 1.414 times the length of a short side. Always. Therefore, for a 1" square, 1" x 1.414 = 1.41"; for a 2" square, 2" x 1.414 = 2.82.

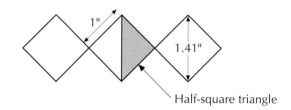

Half-square triangle

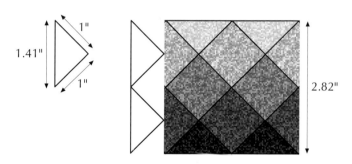

"OK," you say, "but why do we have to use these awkward numbers? Why can't we just round them up or down to quarter inches and go from there?"

Let me explain by example. Say you want to put the Squares on Point border on a large quilt, 90" x 105". We'll do it your way first and call the repeat unit 1½" instead of 1.41". You'll need top and bottom borders 60 squares long (60 x 1½" = 90") and side borders 70 squares long (70 x 1½" = 105"). That was easy.

But the borders won't fit. Using the more accurate repeat unit, 1.41", we can see that the 60-square top and bottom borders will actually be only 84.6" long, and the 70-square side borders will actually be only 98.7" long—too short for a 90" x 105" quilt top.

With a hand calculator, it really isn't any more difficult to work with these numbers than with quarter inches. For example, for the 105" border, divide 105" by the repeat unit 1.41. You'll get another odd number, 74.47", which means you will need 74.47 1" squares for the border. Since you probably don't want a partial square at the end of the border strip, make a border with 75 squares. Then multiply 75 by the repeat unit again to get 75 x 1.41" = 105.75". This is how long the border will be.

You'll need to add to the quilt top to bring it up to the size of the border. Now, if necessary, round the numbers up to eighth inches or quarter inches. (See the chart on page 10.) In this case, to bring the 105"-long quilt sides up to 105¾", add ⅜" to the top edge of the quilt and ⅜" to the bottom (⅜" x ⅜" = ¾") with coping strips.

Coping strips can be as narrow as ¼" or as wide as a few inches. They are often one width for the top and bottom of the quilt top and another width for the sides. Their purpose is to enlarge the quilt top to a size that will fit a whole number of border-design repeats.

Coping strips serve another purpose as well. Even if the pieced border would fit perfectly without them, most quilts look better with coping strips between the pieced quilt top and the pieced border. For example, the 90" top and bottom of our large example quilt will require a border of 64 squares; 64 x 1.41" = 90.24". The border in this case will be only ¼" longer than the quilt. The long edges of the Squares on Point border are entirely bias, and with 90" to work with, you could certainly ease in the extra ¼". However, this would mean no spacer between the quilt top and the pieced border. Instead, let's consider making the border at least one square longer. A border strip with 65 squares would be 91.65" long; by adding coping strips, you can make a 91¾"-wide quilt.

One last point: Because there are many seams in a pieced border, your border will probably turn out slightly longer or shorter than calculated. So first, make all your calculations, sew your pieced borders, and then measure them. If they are longer or shorter than your calculations, increase or decrease the width of the coping strips accordingly. Then cut the coping strips, sew them to the quilt, and add the pieced borders.

Use the following chart to convert decimal fractions to ⅛" and ¼" measurements. Do this conversion after you have calculated the length of your border, to determine the size your quilt must be enlarged to fit the border. Whether you round to the nearest ⅛" or ¼" is up to you. Which is best depends on the situation. For example, I would round a 12"-long border (for a miniature quilt) to the nearest ⅛", and a 90"-long border to the nearest ¼".

Decimal Fraction	*Rounded to nearest ⅛":*
0 to .06"	*0*
.07" to .18"	*⅛" (.125")*
.19" to .31"	*¼" (.25")*
.32" to .43"	*⅜" (.375")*
.44" to .56"	*½" (.5")*
.57" to .68"	*⅝" (.625")*
.69" to .81"	*¾" (.75")*
.82" to .93"	*⅞" (.875")*
.94" to .99"	*1"*

Decimal Fraction	*Rounded to nearest ¼":*
0 to .12"	*0*
.13" to .37"	*¼" (.25")*
.38" to .62"	*½" (.5")*
.63" to .87"	*¾" (.75")*
.88" to .99"	*1"*

CORNERS

Corners have the reputation of being the hardest part of pieced border designs. Corners aren't difficult to construct; the difficult part is getting the borders to end in the right place so each corner smoothly continues the design. Each set of instructions in this book tells you how to sew the corner pieces and how to plan your border so each side begins and ends correctly. Usually, the border must begin and end with a complete repeat unit.

The directions often mention corner squares. A corner square is just that, a square that occupies the corner.

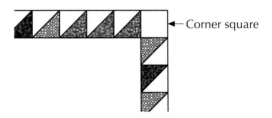

Corner square

Before you make the corners, calculate the border measurements and sew each of the border strips. Sew two opposite border strips to the quilt top, then construct the corner blocks. Sew the corner blocks to the ends of the remaining borders, then sew these borders to the quilt top.

Corner square

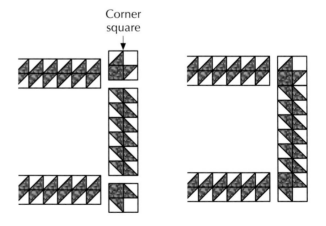

Some borders are pieced so the ends form mitered corners, eliminating separate corner squares. For mitered corners, sew the borders to each side of the quilt top, starting and stopping (and backstitching) ¼" from each corner. Miter the corner seams by stitching from the corner of the quilt top to the outside edge of the border.

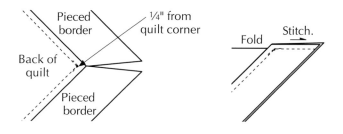

OUTER BORDERS

Just as there is usually a coping strip between the body of the quilt and the pieced border, there is often an outer border strip between the pieced border and the binding. This outer border balances the overall border and also can bring the quilt up to the desired size. "Out of the Blue" (page 20), for example, has a wide outer border that is even wider at the top edge for a pillow tuck. Not all quilts need an outer border; sometimes the binding is enough. Look through the color gallery on pages 13–20 for examples.

SUMMARY
To add a pieced border to your quilt:

1. Measure the length and the width of your quilt top through the center. Subtract ½" to get the finished measurement.
2. Determine the number of repeats of the border design needed for each border strip.
3. Multiply the number of repeats by the length of the repeat unit to determine the actual length of the pieced borders.
4. Determine the width and length of the coping strips needed for the quilt top to fit the borders.
5. Stitch the pieced borders and corners, then measure them.
6. Adjust the width of the coping strips as necessary. Cut the strips and sew them to the quilt top.
7. Sew the pieced borders to the quilt top.
8. Measure the quilt top again and calculate the measurements of the outer borders.
9. Add the outer borders to the quilt top.

Quilting

Pieced borders, like many speed-pieced designs, can be difficult to hand quilt in overall patterns because there are so many seams. I usually quilt pieced borders in-the-ditch, highlighting the design.

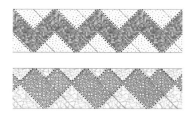

For smaller wall quilts, which I usually quilt only lightly, I may not quilt in the pieced border at all, quilting instead in the unpieced inner and outer border strips.

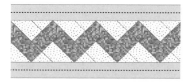

HINT HINT HINT HINT HINT HINT HINT HINT HINT HINT HINT HINT HINT HINT HINT

The chart below indicates which border patterns in this book are strip-pieced, which ones can be foundation-pieced (in smaller sizes), and which ones are good for using up scraps of fabric.

	Page No.	Strip-Pieced	Foundation-Pieced	Scrappy
Easy Braid	28		X	X
Log Cabin Spiral	30		X	X
Flying Geese	32		X	X
Tilted X	34		X	X
Kitty Faces	36			X
Eeek! Mice!	38		X	X
Spinning Stars	40			X
Sawtooth	42		X	X
Double Sawtooth	44		X	X
Stacked Strips	46	X	X	X
Checkerboard	48	X		
Paw Prints	50	X		
Stacked Bricks	53	X		
Squares on Point	56	X		
Beads on a String	58	X		
Small Dogtooth	60	X	X	X
Large Dogtooth	62			X
Folded Ribbon	64	X		
Shaded Squares	66	X		
Arrows	69	X	X	
Zigzag	72	X		
Side-by-Side Hearts	74	X		
Vertical Hearts	76	X		
Twined Border	79	X		
Speed-Pieced Braid	82	X		X
Diamonds	84	X		
Accordion Pleats	87	X		

HINT HINT HINT HINT HINT HINT HINT HINT HINT HINT HINT HINT HINT HINT HINT

GALLERY

Having a Mice Day

by Virginia Morrison, 1995, Seattle, Washington, 41" x 43". Bright mice with embroidered tails and tiny Yo-yo ears have these kitties surrounded. The foundation-pieced cat design is from Janet's book Quilts for Red-Letter Days, That Patchwork Place, Inc. Owned by Anne Kerth.

Puss in Bonnets

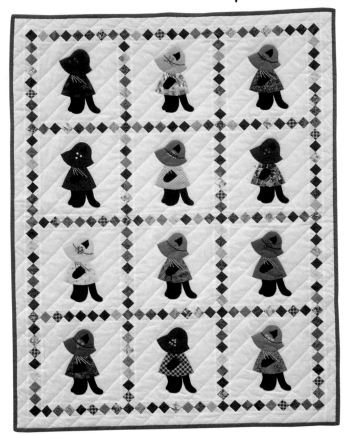

by Virginia Morrison,
1993, Seattle, Washing-
ton, 39" x 50". These
(more or less) traditional
Sunbonnet Sues are both
bordered and sashed with
Squares on Point. The
directions for this quilt are
in *The Cat's Meow* by
Janet Kime, That Patch-
work Place, Inc.

Star Light, Star Bright

by Lorraine Herge,
1996, Concord, North
Carolina, 39" x 39".
The easy strip-pieced
Shaded Squares border
includes several floral
prints for a watercolor
look. Prairie Points
extend the design and
finish the edges.

Emily Launches Her First Fleet

by Karen Gabriel, 1996, Princeton Junction, New Jersey, 41" x 38". Wavelike Log Cabin Spirals border foundation-pieced sailboats. Owned by Emily Kate Wood.

Garden Furrows

by Janet Kime, 1996, Vashon Island, Washington, 30" x 28". Rabbits dressed for work in the garden make up the centers of Log Cabin blocks in the purples, golds, and greens of late summer. The quilt design is the traditional Log Cabin pattern Straight Furrows; the border is simple Stacked Strips.

by Janet Kime and Needle and I friends, 1996, Vashon Island, Washington, 33" x 23". Spring is sprung, the grass is riz…wonder where the flowers is? They're in the Accordian Pleats border.

by Janet Kime, 1996, Vashon Island, Washington, 34" x 16½". Foundation-pieced Flying Geese border these trotting horses. The foundation-pieced horse design is from Janet's book, **Quilts for Red-Letter Days,** *That Patchwork Place, Inc.*

Seattle Stars

by Janet Kime, 1996, Vashon Island, Washington, 64" x 72". These stars in warm reds, cool blues, and soft browns are bordered by a scrappy Double Sawtooth.

Cartoon Kerchoo

by Janet Kime, 1996, Vashon Island, Washington, 24" x 24". This cheerful collection of 1950s hankies, bordered with Spinning Stars, was inspired by the quilts in the book Handkerchief Quilts by Pat Long Gardner, EPM Publications, Inc. Owned by Jared and Kendra Rieger.

Hearts and Flowers

*by Ginne Hooper,
1996, Freehold,
New Jersey,
20" x 20".
Lovely silk-ribbon
embroidery echoes
the Folded Ribbon
border.*

Christmas Sampler

*by Janet Kime and
Needle and I
friends, 1995,
Vashon Island,
Washington, 57" x
57". Three rows
of scrappy Dog-
tooth borders
encircle a set of
Friendship blocks
in this Christmas
lap quilt. Owned
by Kathy and
Marty Clark.*

You Can't Have Too Many Cats

by Janet Kime, 1996, Vashon Island, Washington, 40" x 34½". Cats from Janet's large collection of novelty cat prints are bordered by an Easy Braid in warm browns.

Kittens in the Spools

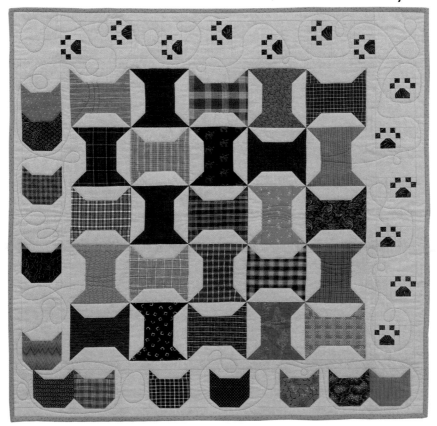

by Janet Kime, 1996, Vashon Island, Washington, 42" x 42". Kittens have been pussyfooting around the spools in this traditional Spool quilt with Kitty Faces and Paw Prints borders. Although Janet's cats have always been wise enough not to eat thread, which can be harmful, the quilted tangles of thread in the borders of this quilt recall the day she returned home to find fifty yards of thread wound around the legs of her sewing-table chair.

by Marie Blichfeldt, 1996, Vashon Island, Washington, 88" x 115". Marie assembled this beautiful sampler quilt in a class taught by Bob Coon, then added a Speed-Pieced Braid border.

HELPFUL HINTS

Border Adventures

If you aren't entirely satisfied with the body of your quilt, you may be able to improve it by being adventuresome with the border. Here are a few ideas for designing pieced borders.

- ✂ If the colors in the quilt top are a little bland, try adding a small amount of something noticeably brighter, darker, or lighter in the border as one of the border-design fabrics or the coping strips.
- ✂ If the colors are a little loud, try toning them down in the border. Use fewer fabrics in the border, or entirely omit one or two of the colors used in the quilt top.
- ✂ If you have used a large-scale print in the body of the quilt, look for a smaller-scale print in similar colors for the border. Or, if prints are all small-scale and the quilt body has an "itsie" look, use a larger-scale print in the border.
- ✂ If the block design just doesn't seem to catch the eye, a pieced border can add interest. The "Zig-zag" border (page 72), for example, looks bold in almost any fabric combination.
- ✂ Echo one of the shapes in the blocks with a larger version in the border. For example, if the blocks have 2" triangles, try 3" triangles in a Sawtooth border.
- ✂ Add a touch of humor to a quilt. See "Kitty Faces" (page 36), "Eeek! Mice!"(page 38), and "Paw Prints" (page 50).

Other Uses

The designs in this book can be used in places other than quilt borders.

- ✂ **Sashing strips.** Pieced sashing strips can enhance many quilts; look at the Squares on Point sashing and borders on "Puss in Bonnets" (page 14). "Flying Geese" (page 32), "Sawtooth" (page 42), "Stacked Strips" (page 46), "Checkerboard" (page 48), and "Squares on Point" (page 56) are easy to plan; "Diamonds" (page 84) is a little more challenging, but worth the effort.

- ✂ **Sampler quilts.** When I teach pieced-border classes, my students often assemble their border strips into samplers. These make attractive wall hangings and small quilts.

- ✂ **Strip quilts.** The strip setting for quilt blocks is an old one, used by our great-grandmothers to stretch a small number of blocks into a quilt. In a strip setting, plain strips of fabric separate long rows of blocks. "Flying Geese," presented as a border in this book, is more often seen as a strip quilt; the same is true of "Easy Braid" (page 28) and "Stacked Bricks" (page 53).

- ✂ A number of other border designs could be used to make an entire quilt top, including "Kitty Faces" (page 36); "Stacked Strips" (page 46); "Large Dogtooth" (page 62), especially when offset in a Zigzag design, see page 61; "Zigzag" (page 72); and "Diamonds" (page 84). "Side-by-Side Hearts" (page 74) or "Vertical Hearts" (page 76) would make a charming miniature quilt.

- ✂ **Clothes.** Experiment with many of the border designs, especially in smaller sizes, for quilted vests and jackets, and as decorative edgings for skirts and other garments. Edge a pocket with a tiny strip of Flying Geese, or make cuffs from a strip of Zigzag.

- ✂ **Pillows and place mats.** The small size and bold designs make the borders ideal for small quilted items that make lovely gifts. Use the borders as decorative edgings for other household items, such as bed sheets and towels.

G E N E R A L
I N S T R U C T I O N S

Fabrics

In general, use 100% cotton fabrics for your quilts. Blends are more difficult to work with; they are slippery, often not as tightly woven, tend to warp out of shape, and don't take a sharp crease. If you mix blends and 100% cottons, the cottons will fade faster; as the quilt mellows, the blends will look harsh.

Rotary Cutting

Except for the small-scale borders that can be foundation-pieced, all the borders in this book are rotary-cut and speed-pieced; there are no templates. You will need at least three pieces of equipment: a rotary cutter, a cutting mat designed for rotary cutters, and one or two transparent acrylic rulers. Don't try to rotary cut without the special mat; you will quickly ruin your blade, not to mention the surface you cut on. Ideally, you should have a mat that is 24" in at least one dimension and a 6" x 24" ruler. A second ruler is not absolutely necessary if your mat has a grid drawn on it, but a 12" ruler or a 6" Bias Square® is handy.

1. Press your fabric before cutting. Fold it with selvages together and lay it on the cutting mat with the fold toward you.

2. If you have a second ruler, place it close to the left edge of the fabric and align it with the fold. Lay the long ruler next to the short ruler so it just covers the raw edges of the fabric. Remove the short ruler.

    If you do not have a second ruler, align the folded edge with a horizontal grid line on the mat. Then line up your long ruler with a vertical grid line so it just covers the raw edges of the fabric.

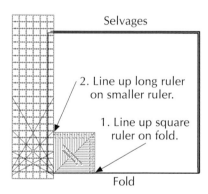

Now cut the fabric with the rotary cutter, rolling the blade away from you, along the side of the long ruler.

This first cut is called a clean-up cut. It tidies the edge of your fabric and ensures that the next cut will be exactly perpendicular to the fold. If the cuts are not perpendicular to the fold, the strips will be crooked when you unfold them. Recheck the angle of the ruler after every two or three cuts, and make another clean-up cut whenever necessary.

3. Now you are ready to cut strips. Align the required measurement on the ruler with the clean-cut edge of the fabric. Cut strips across the width of the fabric, from selvage to selvage, in the required width.

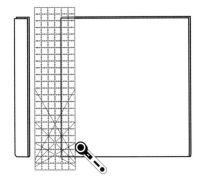

To cut squares:

After cutting strips in the required widths, trim away the selvage ends and crosscut the strips into pieces of the desired size. For example, if your border calls for 4 squares, each 4" x 4", cut a 4"-wide strip across the width of the fabric, fold it, trim the selvages, then make 2 crosscuts, each 4" apart.

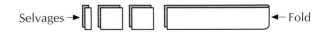

Selvages →   ← Fold

To cut half-square triangles:

Cut a strip ⅞" wider than the *finished* short side of the required triangle to allow for seam allowances. Crosscut a square, then cut the square in half once diagonally. The short sides of a half-square triangle will be on the straight grain of the fabric.

Machine Piecing

Maintaining an exact ¼"-wide seam allowance is essential in machine piecing. If you don't make accurate ¼"-wide seams, the design lines won't match, the triangles won't be pointed, the sections won't fit together properly, and the finished piece won't lie flat.

On many sewing machines, the edge of the presser foot is exactly ¼" from the needle. On some machines, the needle position is movable. On other machines, you will need to make a ¼"-wide seam guide by placing a piece of masking tape on the throat plate.

Test the accuracy of your seam guide by sewing a pieced block and measuring it. Even if you appear to be making accurate ¼"-wide seams, your block may be a little too small. This happens because a little of the fabric is taken up by the bump where each seam allowance is pressed. Most quilters find they need to take a seam allowance that is just a thread or two under ¼". Practice making slight alterations in your seam width until your blocks are consistently the right size.

Pressing

Careful and thorough pressing is one of the most important and neglected aspects of quiltmaking. There are two basic rules of pressing when you machine piece.

1. Press all seam allowances to one side.

Seam allowances are pressed to one side for strength; when seam allowances are pressed open, the stitching is exposed and more subject to wear.

Pressing the seam allowance to one side also allows you to press matching seams in opposite directions; you can then butt seams and more easily match seam lines. In this book, arrows are provided to indicate the direction to press seam allowances. When you have to butt seams several steps later, the seam allowances will already be pressed in opposite directions.

When it is not necessary to butt seams, the pressing arrows indicate the direction that will reduce bulk. When bulk is not an issue, press toward the darker fabric.

2. Press each seam before crossing it with another seam.

   If you do not press a seam flat before crossing it with another seam, a little tuck will form where the seam allowance is folded to one side. Once you cross that tuck with another seam, the tuck is permanently caught in the stitching; no amount of pressing will flatten it. These little tucks will make your block or border smaller than it should be. Discipline yourself to press your seams before proceeding to the next step. After pressing the seam allowance to one side, flip the piece over to the right side, then push the broad side of the iron sideways into the bump of the seam to flatten it.

Speed Piecing

Speed piecing is a combination of rotary-cutting and shortcut-sewing techniques. Many speed-pieced designs require a strip-pieced unit, which is made by sewing fabric strips together lengthwise. The strip-pieced unit is then pressed and crosscut into segments, and the crosscuts are sewn together to make a design.

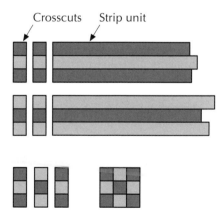

Crosscuts   Strip unit

1. Carefully sew the strips together, with exact ¼"-wide seam allowances, so all finished strip widths are equal. The unit also must be straight; if the bottom fabric feeds into the sewing machine faster than the top fabric or vice versa, the unit will curve. To combat this, sew pairs of strips together from top to bottom, then sew the pairs to each other from bottom to top.

2. Press the strip unit carefully so it lies perfectly flat, with no pleats at the seams. Press the wrong side first. The pattern instructions will tell you which direction to press the seam allowances. Then flip the unit over and press the right side, pushing the broad side of the iron into the bump at each seam, flattening it.

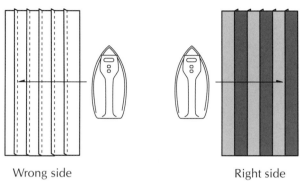

Wrong side   Right side

If the unit curves just slightly, you may be able to steam it back into line. If not, make frequent clean-up cuts as you cut. The crosscuts *must be perpendicular to the seam lines,* or the pieces will not be square.

SPEED-PIECED CORNERS

Several designs in this book use a popular technique for speed piecing triangles to the corners of other pieces.

1. Using a marker and straight edge, draw a diagonal line on the wrong side of the "corner" square. Sew the square to the corner of the other piece, stitching on the diagonal line.

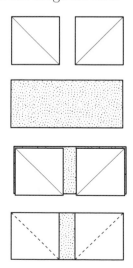

2. Trim the corners, leaving about ¼" for seam allowances. Press the seam allowance toward the corner triangle.

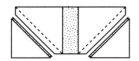

3. If pressing distorts the piece, pull it back into shape by grasping the ends of the stitched diagonal line and pulling gently.

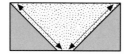

Foundation Piecing

Foundation piecing is a popular technique in which fabric pieces are added, one by one, to a design drawn on a paper or muslin foundation. All seams are sewn directly on the drawn lines, through the foundation. The beauty of foundation piecing is that you can piece very complicated designs without templates. The technique is also useful for miniature designs, where it can be difficult to sew together tiny pieces with accuracy. When you sew the designs using foundation paper, the lines and points are always neat and clean.

If you are new to foundation piecing, try a variety of foundation materials until you find one you like.

- ✂ Tracing paper is my favorite because I can see through it—the drawn design is visible on both sides. I cannot photocopy onto tracing paper, however, so I must trace each line by hand. A good, inexpensive substitute for tracing paper is examination-table paper. Next time you are in for a checkup, ask the nurse if she'll roll off a yard or two for you.
- ✂ Regular paper (typing paper) is a little more difficult to remove after piecing. You also must hold the piece up to the light to see through it. But you can quickly make a number of photocopies of your design.

- ✂ Muslin doesn't have to be removed later, but you can't see through it easily, and I think it wiggles too much. I like the rigidity of paper for greater piecing accuracy.

To foundation-piece:

1. Trace a mirror image of the design as accurately as possible onto the paper or muslin foundation, or photocopy it onto regular paper. Draw a ¼"-wide seam allowance beyond the outer edges of the design. Copy the piece numbers as well; they tell you the order in which to add the pieces. Shade lightly or mark with an X the dark areas of the design to indicate which fabric is used in each section. Cut out the foundation, cutting it a bit larger than the drawn design.

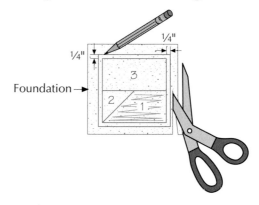

2. Cut a piece of fabric roughly the shape of piece #1 in the design, adding about ¼" all around for a seam allowance. Place the fabric piece, right side up, on the wrong (unmarked) side of the foundation.

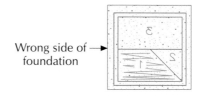

3. Cut a piece of fabric roughly the shape of piece #2 plus seam allowance. Pin it to piece #1, right sides together. Check that both pieces overlap the seam line by at least ¼".

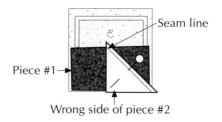

4. Turn the unit over so the printed side of the foundation is facing up and the fabric is on the underside. Sew the seam exactly on the drawn line, extending it ¼" beyond the drawn line on both ends. Do not backstitch at either end.

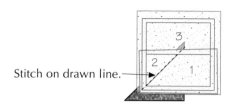

Stitch on drawn line.

5. Turn the unit over so the fabric is on top. Trim the seam allowances to ¼", flip piece #2, and press the seam with a dry iron.

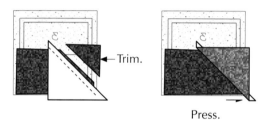

Trim.

Press.

6. Pin piece #3 in place on the wrong side of the foundation, turn the unit over, and sew on the drawn line. Turn the unit over, trim the seam allowances, flip piece #3, and press.

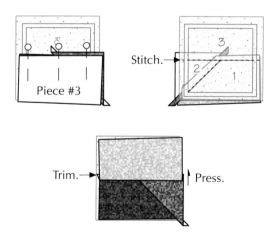

Piece #3

Stitch.

Trim.   Press.

7. For more complex units, add the remaining pieces in numerical order. When all the pieces are sewn, trim the outer edges, leaving a ¼"-wide seam allowance. (Use the outer lines you drew on the pattern for guidance, but use a ruler as a guide when cutting the block to the exact size needed, including ¼"-wide seam allowances.)

8. Leaving the foundation paper in place, sew the borders to the quilt top. Foundation piecing usually results in bias on the outer edge of the border. Wait to remove the foundation paper until after sewing the border to the quilt top. This will prevent the bias edges from stretching. Foundation muslin is never removed.

Enlarging Designs

Unlike templates, which have seam allowances, foundation-pieced designs are easily enlarged with a photocopier. At a photocopy shop, ask them to enlarge the foundation pattern. Before you go, determine the enlargement percentage you will need. For example, if you have a pattern for a 2"-wide border and you want to make it 4" wide, you will need a 200% enlargement.

Embroidery Stitches

A few of the borders in this book may be enhanced with embroidery. Use the simple stitches shown here.

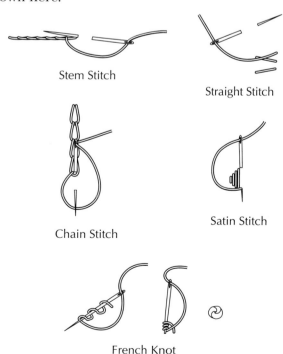

Stem Stitch

Straight Stitch

Chain Stitch

Satin Stitch

French Knot

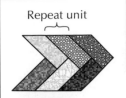

Repeat unit

Finished border width: 3"

Finished size of repeat unit: 1.41"

Easy Braid

The size of this braided border is easy to modify, since it can be constructed of any size rectangle and trimmed to any width. The pattern requires at least three fabrics, but looks best when you use many fabrics and randomly arrange them. This is a good border for using up small scraps of fabric.
If you wish to foundation-piece this border, see page 91.

PLANNING YOUR BORDER

Each ¼ yard of fabric will make about 72 rectangles, each 1½" x 3½", yielding about 50" of border. Estimate the amount of fabric you need from the examples below.

Quilt Size	Total Length of Borders	No. of Rectangles	Braid Fabric
Wall quilt (30" x 45")	150"	230	¾ yd.
Bed quilt (90" x 110")	400"	600	2 yds.

CUTTING AND ASSEMBLY

1. Cut rectangles, each 1½" x 3½".
2. Sew the narrow end of one rectangle to the long side of another as shown. Press.

3. Add the pieces one by one. After each addition, press the seam toward the piece just added.

4. When the braid is the desired length, draw a line down the center of the border on the *wrong* side. Trim the border 1¾" from this center line.

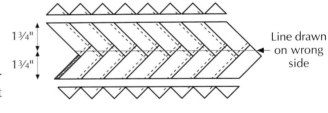

1¾"

1¾"

Line drawn on wrong side

3½"

CORNERS

The corners of this border are mitered. The length of each side of the quilt top before the Easy Braid border is added must be equal to a number of complete repeats. For example:

10 repeats x 1.41" each = 14.1"
22 repeats x 1.41" each = 31.0"

Round the lengths of the borders to the nearest ⅛" or ¼", and add coping strips to bring the quilt top up to the desired measurements. (See "Making a Border That Fits" on pages 7–11.)

1. Sew each border to the length required.
2. Add enough strips to the *right* end of the border so the left end extends a total of 4 strips beyond the edge of the quilt.

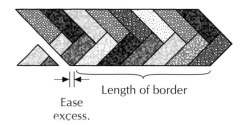

4 extra strips

Length of border

3. Trim the left end of the border even with the raw edge of the top strip as shown. This leaves a fraction of a strip at the base of the left end. (Ease this slight excess on the left end when sewing the border to the quilt.)

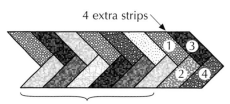

Ease
excess.

Length of border

4. Add strips to the right end and trim even with the long edge of the border as shown.

5. Sew the borders to the quilt top, starting and stopping ¼" from each corner of the quilt top.
6. Miter the corners. (See "Corners" on page 10.)

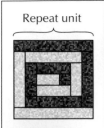

Repeat unit

Finished border width: 5¼"

Finished size of block (repeat unit) 5¼"

Log Cabin Spiral

The blocks that make up the Log Cabin Spiral border are actually "Courthouse Steps," a variation of the Log Cabin block. Selective color placement results in the spiral design. Instead of struggling with narrow strips of fabric, foundation-piece smaller versions of the design. Patterns are on page 91.

PLANNING YOUR BORDER

Plan each border so it includes a number of complete blocks. Each ¼ yard of light fabric and ¼ yard of dark fabric will make about 15 Log Cabin Spiral blocks. Estimate the amount of fabric you need from the examples below.

Quilt Size	Total Length of Borders	No. of Blocks	Light Fabric	Dark Fabric
Wall quilt (30" x 45")	150"	34	⅔ yd.	⅔ yd.
Bed quilt (90" x 110")	400"	82	1½ yds.	1½ yds.

CUTTING AND ASSEMBLY

1. Precut all strips for the blocks, referring to the dimensions given below for each block.

LIGHT LOGS		DARK LOGS	
Log Number	Dimensions	Log Number	Dimensions
1	1¼" x 2"	2	1¼" x 1¼"
3	1¼" x 2¾"	4	1¼" x 2¾"
5	1¼" x 2¾"	6	1¼" x 2¾"
7	1¼" x 4¼"	8	1¼" x 4¼"
9	1¼" x 4¼"	10	1¼" x 4¼"

2. Sew dark log #2 to light log #1.

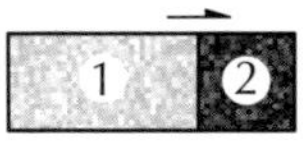

3. Add logs #3 and #4.

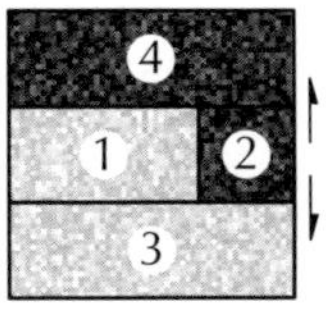

NOTE
Press seam allowances after each seam in the direction of the arrows (always toward the log just added).

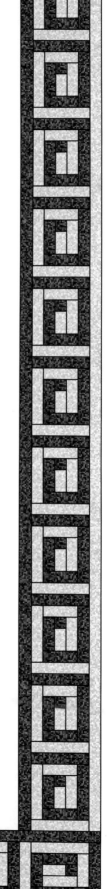

4. Continue adding pairs of logs to opposite sides of the block, pressing after each log. Be careful to add each strip to the correct side of the block, to continue the spiral design.

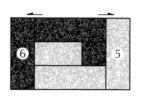

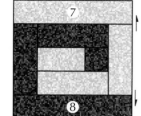

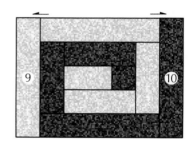

5. Sew the blocks together to make the border strips.
6. For the final logs, cut 1 strip, 1¼" wide and the length of the border, from each of the light and dark fabrics. Sew the strips to the outside edges of each border, continuing the spiral design. (Add the corner blocks to the top and bottom borders *before* this step; see "Corners" below.)

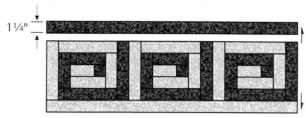

CORNERS

Each border strip must be made of a number of whole Spiral blocks. The finished length of each side of the quilt top before the border is added must be equal to a number of complete Spiral blocks. For example:

10 repeats x 5¼" each = 52.5"
22 repeats x 5¼" each = 115.5"

Adjust this length to the nearest ⅛" or ¼", and add coping strips to bring the quilt top up to the desired measurements. (See "Making a Border That Fits" on pages 7–11.)

CHANGING THE SIZE

The directions given are for 5¼" x 5¼" finished blocks (including the final log strip). The finished logs are ¾" wide. For 7" x 7" finished blocks with 1"-wide finished logs, refer to the chart below.

LIGHT LOGS		DARK LOGS	
Log Number	Dimensions	Log Number	Dimensions
1	1½" x 2½"	2	1½" x 1½"
3	1½" x 3½"	4	1½" x 3½"
5	1½" x 3½"	6	1½" x 3½"
7	1½" x 5½"	8	1½" x 5½"
9	1½" x 5½"	10	1½" x 5½"

VARIATIONS

This border looks best with one light fabric and one dark fabric. To introduce some variation, use a mottled solid-color fabric for the light or dark fabric. (See "Emily Launches Her First Fleet" on page 15.) These fabrics look hand dyed and are now available on bolts, as well as from small companies that hand dye fabrics for quilters.

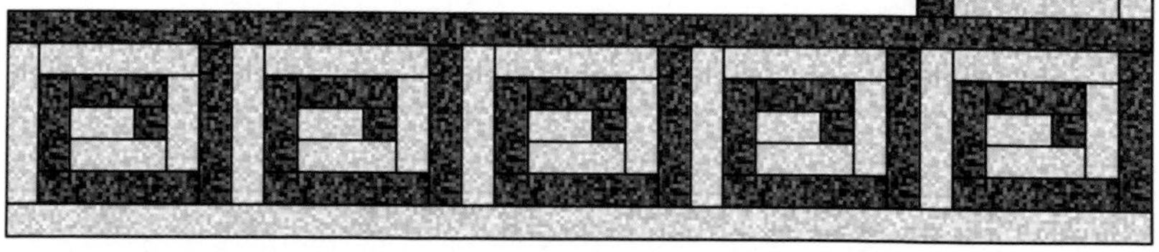

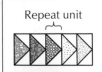

Repeat unit

Finished
border
width:
4"

Finished
size of
repeat
unit:
2"

Flying Geese

Most quilters are familiar with flying-geese units, which can be lined up to make borders and even entire quilts. Flying geese are also part of many pieced blocks. This section includes instructions for flying-geese units in several sizes. The larger sizes are speed-pieced; the smaller sizes can be foundation-pieced, using the patterns on page 92.

PLANNING YOUR BORDER

Each ⅓ yard of geese fabric and ⅓ yard of background fabric will make about 30 flying-geese units. Estimate the amount of fabric you need from the examples below.

Quilt Size	Total Length of Borders	No. of Geese	Geese Fabric	Background Fabric
Wall quilt (30" x 45")	150"	84	¾ yd.	1 yd.
Bed quilt (90" x 110")	400"	208	1¾ yds.	2 yds.

CUTTING AND ASSEMBLY

See "Speed-Pieced Corners" on pages 25–26.

1. For each flying-geese unit, cut 1 rectangle, 2½" x 4½", from geese fabric, and 2 squares, each 2½" x 2½", from background fabric.

2. Speed-piece the background squares to the geese rectangle. If you plan to hand quilt in-the-ditch around the geese, press the seam allowances toward the geese fabric; otherwise, press the seam allowances toward the background fabric.

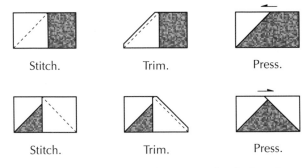

Stitch.   Trim.   Press.

Stitch.   Trim.   Press.

3. Sew the units together to make the borders.

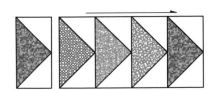

CORNERS

Each border strip should begin and end with a whole flying-geese unit. The finished length of each side of the quilt top before the border is added must be equal to a number of complete repeats. For example:

10 repeats x 2" each = 20"
22 repeats x 2" each = 44"

Add coping strips to bring the quilt top up to the desired measurements. (See "Making a Border That Fits" on pages 7–11.)

1. Sew the side borders to the quilt top.

2. Make corner blocks from 2 flying-geese units, or 1 flying-geese unit and 1 rectangle, 2½" x 4½", of background fabric. Sew the corner blocks to the ends of the top and bottom borders as shown.

3. Sew the top and bottom borders to the quilt top.

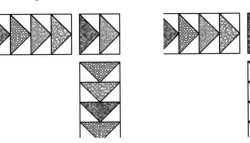

2 flying-geese units   1 flying-geese unit
                             1 rectangle

CHANGING THE SIZE

Refer to the chart below to make flying-geese units in different sizes. Cut pieces from the geese fabric and background fabric according to the dimensions given.

Finished Unit Dimensions	Geese Fabric Dimensions	Background Fabric Dimensions
1¼" x 2½"	1¾" x 3"	1¾" x 1¾"
1½" x 3"	2" x 3½"	2" x 2"
1¾" x 3½"	2¼" x 4"	2¼" x 2¼"
2" x 4"	2½" x 4½"	2½" x 2½"
2½" x 5"	3" x 5½"	3" x 3"
3" x 6"	3½" x 6½"	3½" x 3½"

VARIATIONS

Point the geese in one direction around the quilt.

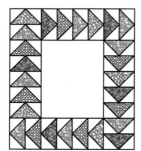

Point the geese toward each other at two opposite corners and away from each other at the two remaining corners. Use squares of background fabric for the corner blocks, or experiment with pieced blocks as shown.

Reverse the direction of the geese at the midpoint of each border so the geese either point toward or away from each other at each corner. Experiment with pieced corner blocks.

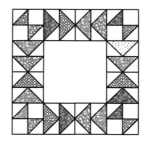

Use one fabric for all the units, select several fabrics for a scrappy border, or alternate two or more fabrics to create a pattern.

Scrappy Geese   Alternating Geese

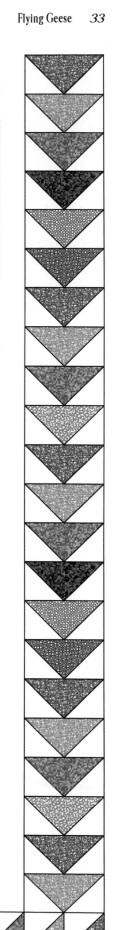

Repeat unit

Finished border width: 3"

Finished size of repeat unit: 3"

Tilted X

This unusual border is open and airy. It's a great way to use up little scraps and can be made from any size of background square. Speed-piece large squares, and foundation-piece smaller squares, using the patterns on page 90.

PLANNING YOUR BORDER

From ¼ yard of X fabric and ½ yard of background fabric, you can make about 42 X squares, yielding about 126" of border. Estimate the amount of fabric you need from the examples below.

Quilt Size	Total Length of Borders	No. of Squares	X Fabric	Background Fabric
Wall quilt (30" x 45")	150"	54	⅓ yd.	½ yd.
Bed quilt (90" x 110")	400"	138	1 yd.	1¼ yds.

CUTTING AND ASSEMBLY

See "Speed-Pieced Corners" on pages 25–26.

1. Cut 3½" x 3½" background squares. From contrasting fabric, cut 2 X-fabric squares, each 2" x 2", for each background square.

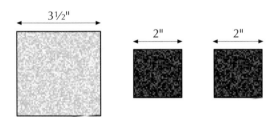

3½"   2"   2"

2. Speed-piece each X square to 2 opposite corners of the background square. Trim the corners ¼" from the stitching and press.

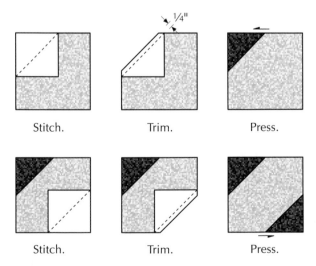

¼"

Stitch.   Trim.   Press.

Stitch.   Trim.   Press.

3. Join the units as shown to make the border.

CORNERS

The length of each side of the quilt top before the Tilted X border is added must be equal to a number of Tilted X repeat units. For example:

10 repeats x 3" each = 30"
22 repeats x 3" each = 66"

Add coping strips to bring the quilt top up to the desired measurements. (See "Making a Border That Fits" on pages 7–11.)

This design is most interesting if the direction of the X is reversed at the midpoint of each border. If the border requires an odd number of units, speed-piece each X square to adjoining corners of a midpoint background square.

Midpoint unit, with 2 adjacent X squares

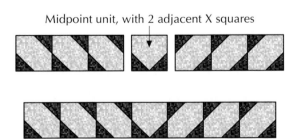

If the border requires an even number of units, speed-piece only 1 X square each to 2 midpoint background squares.

Midpoint units, each with 1 X square

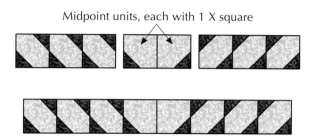

If necessary, adjust the midpoint units to make the borders fit. Begin and end each border with a whole unit.

After you have constructed each border, sew the side borders to the quilt top. Add corner blocks to each end of the top and bottom borders, then sew the borders to the quilt top.

CHANGING THE SIZE

The background squares can be any size. The X squares' finished size is always one-half of the background squares' finished size. For example, if a background square's finished size is 3" x 3", the finished size of the X squares will be 1½" x 1½". After adding ½" to each side for seam allowances, cut the background squares 3½" x 3½" and the X squares 2" x 2".

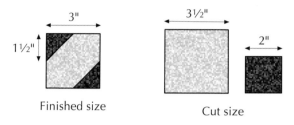

Finished size   Cut size

VARIATIONS

Cut the X squares from many fabrics for a scrappy border.

If you want each X in the border to be one fabric, stack the X squares in pairs. Sew each pair's first square to the bottom corner of a background square, and the second square to the top corner of the next background square.

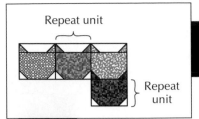

Repeat unit

} Repeat unit

Finished border width: 3"

Finished size of horizontal repeat unit: 3"

Finished size of vertical repeat unit: 2¼"

Kitty Faces

These simple kitty faces can interlock in the side borders and nestle side by side in the top and bottom borders. Or, if you would like a more open design, you can insert background spacers between the units. Unless you have spacers, use at least two alternating fabrics so each kitty is distinct from its neighbors.

PLANNING YOUR BORDER

Each ⅓ yard of kitty fabric and ¼ yard of background fabric will make about 40 kitty faces, yielding about 120" of horizontal border, or about 90" of vertical border. Estimate the amount of fabric you need from the examples below.

Quilt Size	Total Length of Borders	No. of Kitties	Kitty Fabric	Background Fabric
Wall quilt (30" x 45")	150"	64	⅔ yd.	¼ yd.
Bed quilt (90" x 110")	400"	162	1⅔ yds.	¼ yd.

CUTTING AND ASSEMBLY

See "Speed-Pieced Corners" on pages 25–26.

1. For each kitty-face unit, cut the following:

Fabric	No. of Pieces	Dimensions
Kitty (ears)	2	1¼" x 1¼"
(face)	1	2¾" x 3½"
Background	1	1¼" x 3½"
	2	1¼" x 1¼"

2. Speed-piece a 1¼" x 1¼" kitty ear to each end of a 1¼" x 3½" background strip. Trim the corners and press.

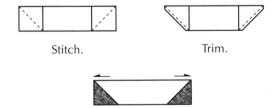

Stitch.　　　Trim.

Press.

3. Speed-piece a 1¼" background square to each lower corner of a 2¾" x 3½" kitty face. Trim and press.

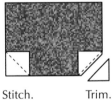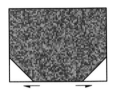

Stitch.　　Trim.　　　Press.

4. Sew the ear unit to the face unit as shown. Sew kitty-face units into horizontal rows for the top and bottom borders.

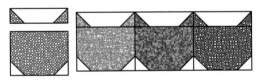

Top and Bottom Borders

5. For each side border, make 1 ear unit from step 2, then repeat step 3, but substitute the ear squares of the next kitty below for the 1¼" background squares. This interlocks each kitty-face unit to the next one in the vertical row.

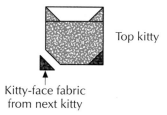

Top kitty

Kitty-face fabric
from next kitty

6. Continue sewing side-border kitty-face units. For the bottom unit, substitute 2 background squares at the lower corners instead of ear squares. Sew units into vertical rows for the side borders.

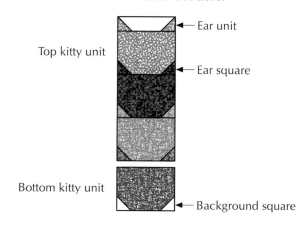

Top kitty unit

Ear unit

Ear square

Bottom kitty unit

Background square

CORNERS

In the side borders, the repeat unit is 2¼" long. The finished length of the side of your quilt must be a multiple of 2¼" minus ¾". For example:

10 repeats x 2¼" each = 22½"
22½" – ¾" = 21¾"

Construct the side borders for the number of interlocking kitty-face units calculated (10 in the example). Then add 1 kitty-face unit at the top and 1 at the bottom of each side bor-

der for the corners. Sew the top and bottom borders to the quilt top first, then add the side borders.

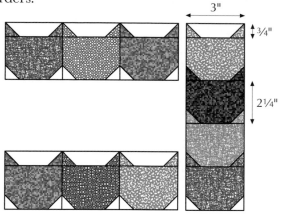

3"

¾"

2¼"

CHANGING THE SIZE

Refer to the chart below to make 4" x 4" (finished size) kitty-face units.

Fabric	No. of Pieces	Dimensions
Kitty (ears)	2	1½" x 1½"
(face)	1	3½" x 4½"
Background	1	1½" x 4½"
	2	1½" x 1½"

VARIATIONS

Use two alternating fabrics for the kitty faces, or use a number of fabrics for a scrappy border. You can even have a few calico cats with mismatched ears.

If you put background spacers between the kitty faces, as in "Kittens in the Spools" (page 19), you could cut all of the cats from the same fabric.

You can embroider eyes and whiskers on some or all of the kitty faces.

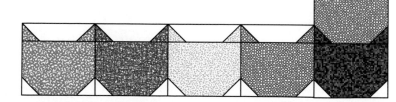

Repeat unit

Finished border width: 3"

Finished size of repeat unit: 4½"

Eeek! Mice!

Send these little mice scurrying around the borders of a child's quilt or your favorite cat blocks.
For smaller mice, use the foundation-piecing patterns on page 93.

PLANNING YOUR BORDER

Each ¼ yard of mouse fabric and ¾ yard of background fabric will make about 48 mice, yielding about 216" of border. Each ¼ yard of contrasting fabric will make about 80 mouse ears (or use scraps). Estimate the amount of fabric you need from the examples below.

Quilt Size	Total Length of Borders	No. of Mice	Mice Fabric	Background Fabric
Wall quilt (30" x 45")	150"	34	¼ yd.	½ yd.
Bed quilt (90" x 110")	400"	90	½ yd.	1¼ yds.

CUTTING AND ASSEMBLY

See "Speed-Pieced Corners" on pages 25–26.

1. For each mouse, cut the following:

Fabric	No. of Pieces	Dimensions
Mouse	1	2" x 3½"
Background	2	2" x 2"

2. Speed-piece a background square to 1 end of each mouse rectangle. Trim and press as shown.

Stitch.　　　Trim.　　　Press.

3. Join the mouse units end to end, adding a background square between each mouse unit.

4. Cut a 2"-wide strip of background fabric the length of each border and add to the top of each border strip.

2"

5. Each mouse ear is a fabric Yo-yo. Using the Yo-yo template on page 39, cut 1 circle of contrasting fabric for each mouse. Turn the edge under ⅛" and sew with a running stitch. Pull up the stitches to gather; tie off.

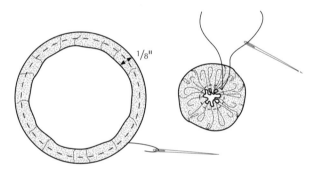

¹/₈"

6. Attach the Yo-yo ears, gathered side down, and stitch the mouse tails, using the embroidery pattern on page 39. (See "Embroidery Stitches" on page 27.) Embroider the tail of the last mouse on each border after you add the corner squares and attach the border to the quilt top.

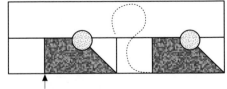

Embroider last mouse's tail after adding borders.

CORNERS

Each border should be made from a number of complete mice. The finished length of each side of the quilt top before the border is added must be equal to a number of complete repeats. For example:

10 repeats x 4½" each = 45"
22 repeats x 4½" each = 99"

Add coping strips to bring the quilt top up to the desired measurements. (See "Making a Border That Fits" on pages 7–11.)

1. Sew the side borders to the quilt top.
2. Add one 3½" background square to each end of the top and bottom borders.

3. Sew the top and bottom borders to the quilt top.
4. Embroider the tails on the last mice.

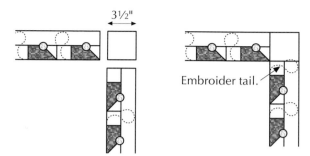

3½"

Embroider tail.

CHANGING THE SIZE

Use the chart below to make larger mice. Cut the long background strip the same width as the background squares.

Repeat Unit	Border Width Dimensions	Mouse Fabric Dimensions	Background Fabric*
6"	4"	2½" x 4½"	2½" x 2½"
7½"	5"	3" x 5½"	3" x 3"

*Cut 2 background squares per mouse.

VARIATIONS

The mice can all face the same direction, so they look like they're running in a circle around the quilt. Or, reverse the direction in the middle of each border, so they face each another in the center of each border. (See "Having a Mice Day" on page 13.)

To adjust the length of the border, make the background squares between the mice wider or narrower. They can even be made different sizes so the mice are spaced randomly around the border.

This is a good border for using little scraps of fabric to make each mouse different. You can use scraps of different colors of embroidery floss for the tails.

Try substituting buttons or appliquéd circles for the Yo-yo ears.

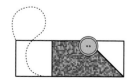

Tail
Embroidery
Pattern

Yo-Yo Template

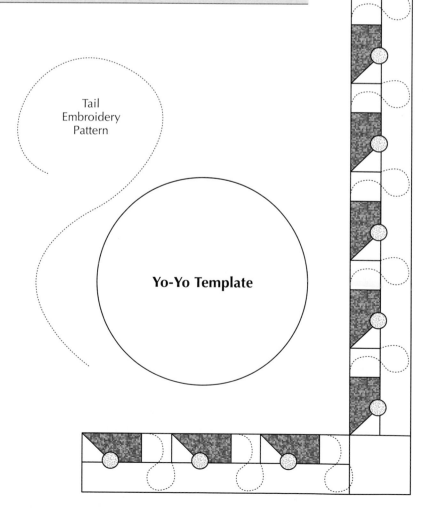

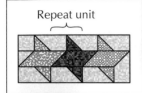

Repeat unit

Finished border width: 3"

Finished size of repeat unit: 2" plus 1"

Spinning Stars

These simple stars are speed-pieced in three strips. Because the stars aren't strip-pieced, the border is a good one for using up little scraps of fabric.

PLANNING YOUR BORDER

Each ¼ yard of star fabric and ¼ yard of background fabric will make about 30 stars, yielding about 60" of border. Estimate the amount of fabric you need from the examples below.

Quilt Size	Total Length of Borders	No. of Stars	Star Fabric	Background Fabric
Wall quilt (30" x 45")	150"	78	⅔ yd. total	½ yd.
Bed quilt (90" x 110")	400"	202	1½ yds. total	1¼ yds.

CUTTING AND ASSEMBLY

See "Speed-Pieced Corners" on pages 25–26.

1. Cut the following pieces:

Fabric	No. of Pieces		Dimensions
	Each Star	Total for Corners	
Star	1		1½" x 3½"
	2		1½" x 1½"
Background	2		1½" x 2½"
		10	1½" x 1½"
		2	1½" x 2½"
		2	1½" x 3½"

You will piece the middle border strips first and use them to establish the order of the fabrics. Then you can match the inner and outer star-point strips to the middle border strips.

For your quilt's top and bottom borders, you will piece the number of stars needed. For each of the side borders, you'll piece the number of stars needed plus one star.

2. For the middle border strip, speed-piece the star-fabric rectangles end to end. Do not press the seams yet.

Stitch.   Trim.

3. Speed-piece a background square to each end of the finished strips as shown. Press the seam allowances in opposite directions from seam to seam, proceeding in this manner all around the border.

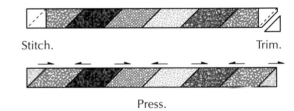

Stitch.   Trim.

Press.

4. For the inner and outer star points, speed-piece 1 star-fabric square to each 1½" x 2½" background rectangle for all stars. Sew these star points together end to end as shown, matching the order of fabrics to the middle strip. Press the seam allowances toward the star fabrics. (If you don't plan to hand quilt, press the 90° end-to-end seam allowances away from the star fabric.)

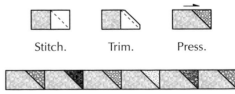

Stitch.   Trim.   Press.

5. At the ends of the inner and outer star-point strips, trim the background fabric and add

background rectangles where indicated in the diagram.

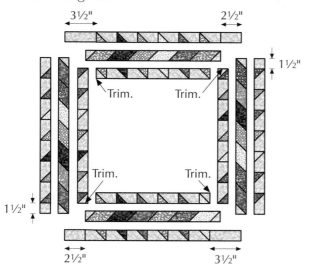

CORNERS

Because the stars overlap, each border will include a number of 2" repeats plus 1" to finish the last star. For example, a border strip of 23 stars will be 46" + 1" = 47" long.

To determine the number of stars you need, divide the length of each side of your quilt by the repeat measurement and round up. Total up the 4 sides, then add 2 stars for the corners. For example, to border an 83" x 95" quilt:

83" ÷ 2" = 41½ stars = 42 stars
95" ÷ 2" = 47½ stars = 48 stars
42 top + 42 bottom + 48 side + 48 side + 2 for corners = 182 stars

1. Sew the top and bottom inner strips to the quilt top, then add the side inner strips. Press the seam allowances toward the quilt top. Sew the top and bottom middle strips to the quilt top, then add the side middle strips. Press the seam allowances toward the middle strips.

2. Sew the side outer strips to the quilt top, then add the top and bottom outer strips. Press the seam allowances toward the middle strips.

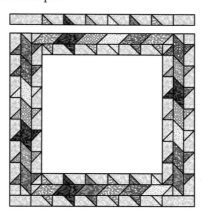

CHANGING THE SIZE

Because the stars overlap, the repeat unit is less than one whole star; it is actually two-thirds of a star. The easiest star sizes to work with are those divisible by 3, such as 3", 4½", and 6" squares.

VARIATIONS

Use just one fabric for the stars, and alternate the star fabric with background fabric in the middle strip. For 3" stars, sew 1½" x 4½" background rectangles (instead of the 1½" x 2½" rectangles) to the star-point squares. Line up the stars with the inside edges of the quilt, and finish the corners with plain 3½" background squares.

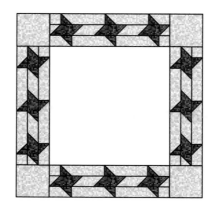

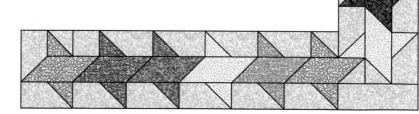

Repeat unit

Finished border width: 2"

Finished size of repeat unit: 2"

Sawtooth

This basic border should be in everyone's repertoire. It complements all the traditional pieced designs that include half-square triangles. The repeat unit is small and—unlike many border designs—is a nice, even, easily manipulated measurement. Best of all, there are many ways to vary the design of the border and the corners.

Miniature Sawtooth borders are difficult to speed-piece accurately. Foundation-piece them, using the patterns on page 93, or draw the size you need on graph paper.

PLANNING YOUR BORDER

From ¼ yard of Sawtooth fabric and ¼ yard of background fabric, you can make about 84 Sawtooth units, each 2" x 2", yielding about 168" of border. Estimate the amount of fabric you need from the examples below.

Quilt Size	Total Length of Borders	Sawtooth Fabric	Background Fabric
Wall quilt (30" x 45")	150"	¼ yd.	¼ yd.
Bed quilt (90" x 110")	400"	¾ yd.	¾ yd.

CUTTING AND ASSEMBLY

This border is assembled from half-square triangle units, sewn together side by side.

There are many methods for speed piecing large numbers of half-square triangle units. If you plan to use only one Sawtooth fabric in your border, consult one of the many That Patchwork Place, Inc., publications that describe these methods, such as *Rotary Riot* by Judy Hopkins and Nancy J. Martin or *Simply Scrappy Quilts* by Nancy J. Martin.

I like to include many fabrics in my Sawtooth borders, and I use the following method. It's not particularly fast, but it produces accurate Sawtooth units and allows me to use many background fabrics as well as many Sawtooth fabrics.

1. Cut 3" squares of background and Sawtooth fabrics.

2. Draw a diagonal line on the wrong side of each background square.

3. Place a square of background fabric and a square of Sawtooth fabric right sides together. Stitch a scant ¼" from each side of the drawn line.

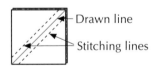

Drawn line

Stitching lines

4. Cut apart on the drawn line. Press the seam allowances toward the darker fabric.

5. Place the diagonal line of a Bias Square on the seam and trim the unit to 2½" x 2½".

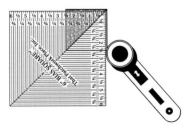

CORNERS

Each border strip must begin and end with a whole Sawtooth unit. The finished length of each side of the quilt top, before the Sawtooth border is added, must be equal to a number of complete units. For example:

10 repeats x 2" each = 20"
22 repeats x 2" each = 44"

Add coping strips to bring the quilt top up to the desired measurements. (See "Making a Border That Fits" on pages 7–11.)

Assemble the side Sawtooth borders and join them to the quilt top. Then add the corner squares to the ends of the top and bottom borders, and sew these borders to the quilt top.

Although you can extend the Sawtooth units from edge to edge, Sawtooth corners usually include squares of background fabric. (See "Variations" below.)

CHANGING THE SIZE

If there are small half-square triangles in your quilt, you will probably want to make the triangles in your Sawtooth border the same size. If you want to use the method described here to make the Sawtooth units, cut the squares 1" larger than the finished size of the triangles. (The finished size is the finished measurement of a short side of the triangle.) For example, if the finished size of the triangles is 3½", cut the squares 4½" x 4½".

VARIATIONS

For such simple units, there is a surprising number of ways to arrange them into a Sawtooth border. Pay particular attention to the corners of the examples.

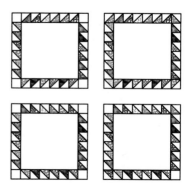

The Sawtooth units can change direction in the center of the border. If you have an even number of Sawtooth units, point half in one direction and half in the other.

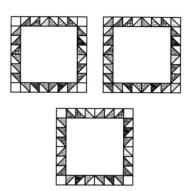

If you have an odd number of Sawtooth units, place a square of background fabric in the center.

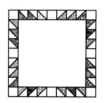

If you like, appliqué or embroider something in the center of the border, or add a small pieced block. This square of background fabric can be a handy coping square; make it wider or narrower, if necessary, to make your pieced border fit.

You can make the Sawtooth units all from the same fabric, or you can make them scrappy. Or, you can arrange two or more fabrics in a repeating design.

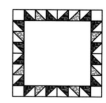

Repeat unit

Finished
border
width:
4"

Finished
size of
repeat
unit:
2"

Double Sawtooth

Double Sawtooth is just what it sounds like: two rows of Sawtooth units. Just as with the single Sawtooth, many variations are possible. Use the foundation-piecing patterns on page 93 for smaller versions.

CUTTING AND ASSEMBLY

Follow the instructions for the Sawtooth border on pages 42–43.

VARIATIONS

In the basic version of the Double Sawtooth, each border strip is made of two identical single Sawtooth strips (one rotated 180°) and joined to make diamond shapes.

Rotate.

Each corner block includes 2 additional Sawtooth units and 2 squares, each 2½" x 2½", one of background fabric and one of Sawtooth fabric.

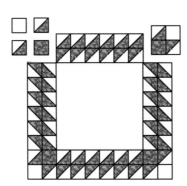

Another version of the Double Sawtooth is made of two rows of single Sawtooth units, one below the other. The corner squares can be 4½" background squares, or they can be pieced as shown.

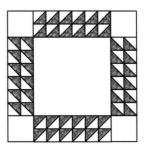

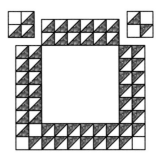

As with the single Sawtooth, the direction of the units can be reversed in the center of each border. Use background-fabric or pieced corner squares.

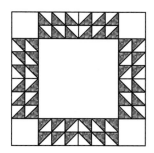

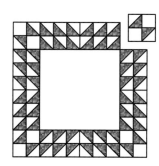

You can also separate the two rows of units with a 1½"-wide strip of Sawtooth or background fabric. To piece the corner blocks as shown, cut the background rectangles 1½" x 2½". Cut the large corner squares 3½" x 3½".

1½" x 2½"→

←2½" x 2½"

3½" x 3½"

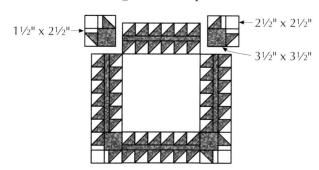

1½" x 2½"

1½" x 4½"→

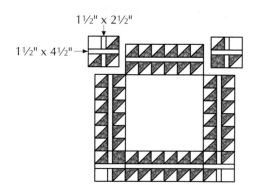

To make this corner version,
cut the background rectangles
1½" x 2½" and 1½" x 4½".

Sawtooth units can also be arranged in a Flying Geese design. This is particularly effective when many fabrics are used.

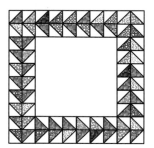

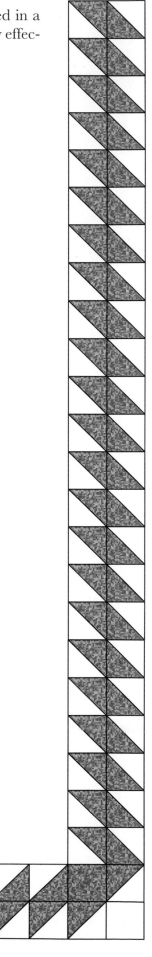

Repeat unit

Finished border width: 3"

Finished size of repeat unit: 1"

Stacked Strips

One of the easiest borders to speed-piece, this border was also a favorite of our great-grandmothers for using up skinny scraps of fabric. Use the foundation-piecing patterns on page 90 to piece smaller borders, or use lined or graph paper.

PLANNING YOUR BORDER

Each ¼ yard of fabric will make about 72" of border. Estimate the amount of fabric you need from the examples below.

Quilt Size	Total Length of Borders	No. of 1½" x 44" Strips	Total Fabric
Wall quilt (30" x 45")	150"	13	⅔ yd.
Bed quilt (90" x 110")	400"	34	1½ yds.

CUTTING AND ASSEMBLY

See "Speed Piecing" on pages 25–26.

1. Cut 1½"-wide strips of a variety of fabrics and sew them together lengthwise into strip units. Use as many strips for each strip unit as you are comfortable working with; however, it is easiest to keep the strip unit less than 22" wide so you can make the crosscuts without having to fold the unit.

2. Make 3½"-wide crosscuts.

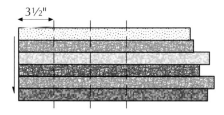

3½"

3. Join the crosscuts end to end to make borders the correct length.

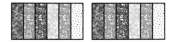

4. If the borders are slightly long, resew a few seams, taking a slightly larger seam allowance. (It isn't necessary to rip out the old seam first.) If the borders are slightly short, rip out a few seams and resew them, taking a slightly smaller seam allowance.

CORNERS

Use 3½" squares of one of the border fabrics for the corner squares.

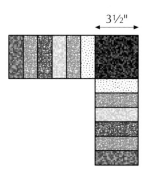

3½"

Instead of plain corner squares, you may want to use pieced blocks.

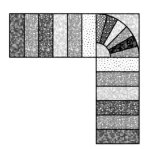

Sew the side borders to the quilt top. Add the corner squares to each end of the top and bottom borders, then sew these borders to the quilt top.

If you prefer, you can miter the corners. Sew each border the length of the side of the quilt top plus twice the finished width of the border. For example, if the side of the quilt top is 54½" long and the border is 3" wide, make the border 54½" + 3" + 3" = 60½" long.

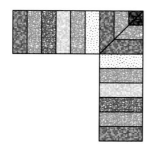

CHANGING THE SIZE

This is an easy border to modify; the strips can be any width and any length. If you want to make your quilt longer, make the top and bottom Stacked Strip borders wider than the side Stacked Strip borders. If the blocks in your quilt include strips (such as Log Cabin blocks), you may want to cut strips for your border units the same width as those in your quilt.

VARIATIONS

Instead of a scrappy border, alternate strips cut from two or more fabrics to create a repeating design.

You can also cut the strips from a shaded series of fabrics.

For another variation, cut the strips in a variety of widths.

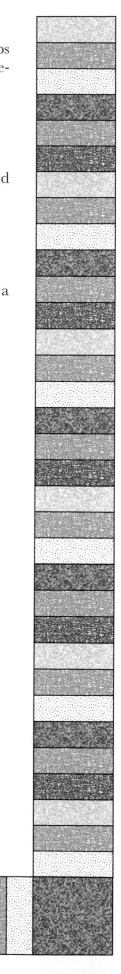

Repeat unit

Finished border width: 2"

Finished size of repeat unit: 1"

Checkerboard

This is a fun border to strip-piece and is especially effective on folk-art and primitive-style quilts. Children like it too. Use two contrasting fabrics for a bold border, or two similar colors for a more subtle check.

PLANNING YOUR BORDER

Each 8-strip unit will make about 112" of border. Estimate the amount of fabric you need from the examples below.

Quilt Size	Total Length of Borders	No. of Strip Units	Dark Fabric	Light Fabric
Wall quilt (30" x 45")	150"	1½	⅓ yd.	⅓ yd.
Bed quilt (90" x 110")	400"	4	¾ yd.	¾ yd.

CUTTING AND ASSEMBLY

See "Speed Piecing" on pages 25–26.

1. Cut dark and light strips, each 1½" wide, and sew them into a strip unit, alternating dark and light. You can actually sew any number of strips together, as long as you start the strip unit with one color and end with the other. Make the unit no more than 22" tall so you won't have to fold the unit to crosscut it. Press all seam allowances in one direction.

2. Make 1½"-wide crosscuts.

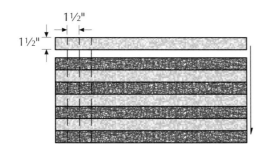

1½"

1½"

3. Join crosscuts end to end to make the length needed for each border. Where necessary, rip out a seam between squares to make the border the correct length. Sew the strips together so the seam allowances are all pressed in one direction in each long strip.

Discard.

4. Sew 2 strips together lengthwise to make a border 2 rows wide. Align the strips so their seam allowances are pressed in opposite directions.

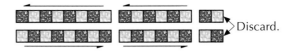

CORNERS

The corners are simply extensions of the border. To maintain the checkerboard pattern, either all four borders must contain an even number of squares, or all four borders must contain an odd number of squares. For example, using 1" finished squares, all four borders must be an even number of inches (for example, 18", 52", 96"), or all four borders must be an odd number of inches (for example, 19", 53", 97").

Assemble your borders, starting on one side and working around the quilt. For example, start with the right side, then assemble the bottom, left side, and finally, the top. As you go, be sure to maintain the alternating light/dark of the checkerboard pattern. Extend the top and bottom borders at each end to make the corner squares. After assembling the borders, sew the side borders to the quilt, then add the top and bottom borders.

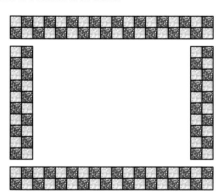

CHANGING THE SIZE

Cut strips the width of the finished size of your squares plus ½". For example, if you want 2" squares, cut your strips 2½" wide. The width of the crosscuts is the same as the cut width of the individual strips. The finished border width will be twice the finished width of your squares.

VARIATIONS

For a scrappy border, assemble several strip units from a variety of light and dark fabrics. If you need only a few strip units for your quilt, make shorter strip units that are 22" (or even 11") long instead of 44".

Make your border wider by sewing together three or more rows of strips.

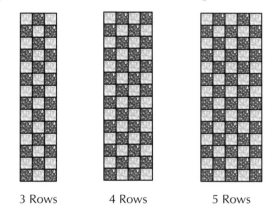

3 Rows   4 Rows   5 Rows

> **HINT HINT HINT HINT HINT HINT**
>
> *For a miniature quilt, use checkered print fabric instead of piecing a Checkerboard border. The narrow inner border on "Garden Furrows" (page 15) is also made from checkered fabric.*

Repeat unit

Finished
border
width:
4"

Finished
size of
repeat
unit:
5"

Paw Prints

This border looks like someone has been pussyfooting around your quilt. Instructions are provided for small paw prints that you can use for wall hangings, and larger paw prints you can use for bed quilts.

PLANNING YOUR BORDER

Each set of strip units makes about 42 paw prints, yielding about 210" of border. Estimate the amount of fabric you need from the examples below.

Quilt Size	Total Length of Borders	Paw Print Repeats*	No. of Strip Units	Paw Print Fabric	Background Fabric
Wall quilt (30" x 45")	150"	34	1	¼ yd.	1 yd.
Bed quilt (90" x 110")	400"	84	2	½ yd.	1⅔ yds.

*Paw-print unit plus a 3½" x 4½" background rectangle

CUTTING AND ASSEMBLY

See "Speed Piecing" on pages 25–26.

1. Construct strip units A and B, cutting strips the widths shown in the diagram. Press all seam allowances as indicated.
2. Make 1"-wide crosscuts.

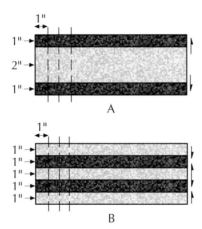

3. Sew the crosscuts together in pairs to make the top half of each paw print. Press.

4. For the bottom of each paw print, cut:

Fabric	No. of Pieces	Dimensions
Paw print	1	1½" x 2"
Background	2	1" x 1"
	2	1" x 1½"

5. Speed-piece 1 background square to 2 adjacent corners of the paw-print rectangle as shown. Add the 2 background rectangles to each end of this unit. Sew the paw-print top to the paw-print bottom. Press.

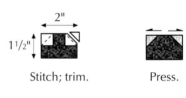

Stitch; trim.   Press.

6. If you prefer to foundation-piece the paw-print bottom, use the pattern provided.

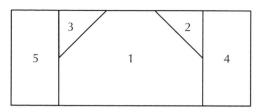

Paw-Print Bottom
Foundation Pattern

7. Sew a 2" x 2½" background rectangle to the right end of half of the paws, and to the left end of the remaining paws.

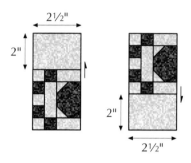

8. Sew 3½" x 4½" background spacers between the paw prints.

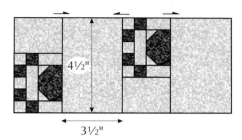

CORNERS

Refer to the border diagram at right for the placement of the paw prints and background spacers as you go around the corners. Orient the paw prints so they make a continuous trail around the quilt. The background spacer between the paw prints can be wider or narrower to help fit the borders to your quilt top; the width of the spacers can even vary between paw prints.

Sew the top and bottom borders to the quilt top. Add background spacers to the ends of the side borders, then sew the side borders to the quilt top.

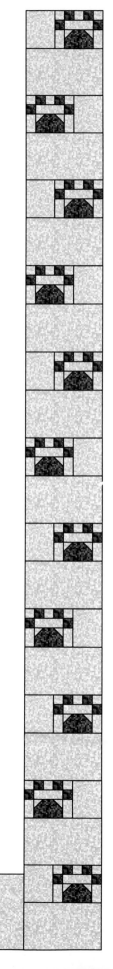

CHANGING THE SIZE

For paw prints that are twice as large (4" x 5"), follow the measurements in the chart below. This border's finished size is 8" wide with a 10" repeat.

Fabric	Large Paw Print No. of Pieces	Dimensions
Strip Unit A		
Paw print	2	1½" x 42"
Background	1	3½" x 42"
Strip Unit B		
Paw print	2	1½" x 42"
Background	3	1½" x 42"
Paw-Print Bottom Rectangle (each)		
Paw print	1	2½" x 3½"
Background	2	1½" x 1½"
	2	1½" x 2½"
	1	3½" x 4½"
Background Spacer	1 per paw print	6½" x 8½"

Each set of strip units makes about 280" of border. Estimate the amount of fabric you need from the example below.

Quilt Size	Total Length of Borders	Paw Print Repeats*	No. of Strip Unit Sets	Paw Print Fabric	Background Fabric
Bed quilt (90" x 110")	400"	44	1½	¾ yd.	3½ yds.

*Paw-print unit plus a 6½" x 8½" rectangle

VARIATIONS

You can make the border wider by increasing the width of the background rectangle next to each paw print. In the second example below, the pieces are cut 3" wide instead of 2", increasing the finished width of the border to 5" instead of 4".

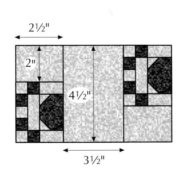
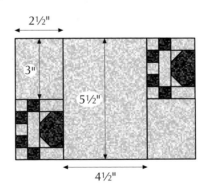

Stacked Bricks

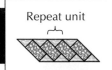

This easy border is a classic Seminole strip-pieced design. It makes an especially nice border for a scrappy quilt. Cut some bricks in a few different sizes (several of each), and lay them along the edge of your quilt top to determine the best border dimensions for your quilt.

Finished border width: 3.18"

Finished size of repeat unit: 2.12"

PLANNING YOUR BORDER

Each strip unit will make about 45" of border. Estimate the amount of fabric you need from the examples below.

Quilt Size	Total Length of Borders	No. of Strip Units	Brick Fabric	Background Fabric
Wall quilt (30" x 45")	150"	4	½ yd.	⅔ yd.
Bed quilt (90" x 110")	400"	9½	1¼ yds.	1⅓ yds.

CUTTING AND ASSEMBLY

See "Speed Piecing" on pages 25–26.

1. Construct a strip unit, cutting the strips the widths shown in the diagram. Press the seam allowances as indicated. Draw a line down the center of the strip unit, on the wrong side of the brick fabric. Make 2"-wide crosscuts.

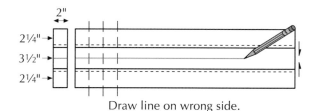

Draw line on wrong side.

2. Join pairs of crosscuts, matching the seam of one to the drawn line on the other as shown. Stagger the crosscuts *down* for 2 borders (opposite sides of the quilt), and stagger them *up* for the remaining 2 borders (top and bottom).

Match seam with drawn line.

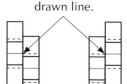

Stagger 2 borders down and 2 borders up.

3. Sew the pairs into fours, and the fours into eights, continuing until the borders are long enough for the quilt top. Press the seam allowances in one direction, pressing carefully to avoid distorting the bias edges.

4. Trim the long edges, leaving a ¼"-wide seam allowance.

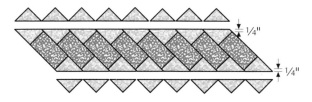

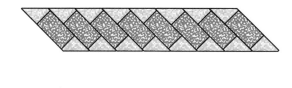

CORNERS

Each border strip begins and ends with one whole crosscut. The finished length of each side of the quilt top before the border is added must be equal to a number of complete repeats. For example:

10 repeats x 2.12" each = 21.2"
22 repeats x 2.12" each = 46.6"

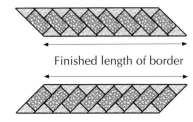

Finished length of border

Adjust the length of the borders to the nearest ⅛" or ¼", and add coping strips to bring the quilt top up to the desired measurements. (See "Making a Border That Fits" on pages 7–11.)

The bricks are staggered *up* in the top and bottom borders, and *down* in the side borders. (See illustration at right.)

Sew all four borders to the quilt top, starting and stopping ¼" from each corner. Two opposite corners are simple miters (see page 11). For the other two corners, construct finishing triangle units as shown.

1. Cut two 2" x 6½" bricks. Sew one 2" background square to each end. Cut one 3⅞" square in half once diagonally to make the background triangles.

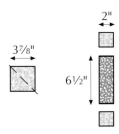

2. Center, then sew 1 regular brick crosscut to the unit made in step 1, and add 1 background triangle. Trim as shown.

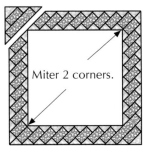

Brick Crosscut   Trim.   Make 2.

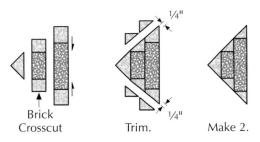

Miter 2 corners.

To make all four corners identical, reverse the direction of the bricks in the center of each row. *Note that on each border, half the bricks are staggered up and half are staggered down.*

1. Make a triangle unit for the center of each border. Cut a 2" brick fabric square and a 2⅜" background square. Cut the background square in half once diagonally to make 2 triangles.

2⅜"   2"

2. Remove a background triangle from one of the border halves as shown and discard. Sew the triangle unit to this border half. Add the other half of the border.

Remove.

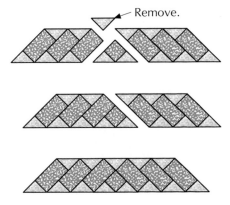

3. Make 4 finishing triangle units, following steps 1 and 2 of "Corners" at left.

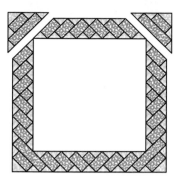

Add finishing triangle units.

CHANGING THE SIZE

The bricks can be rectangles of almost any size. Once you have decided on the finished dimensions of the bricks, add ½" to the *length* for seam allowances. Cut the brick fabric strip this wide. Add ½" to the *width* of the finished rectangle to determine the crosscut width. Cut the background strips ½" wider than the crosscut width.

For example, if you want your finished bricks to be 3" x 5", cut the brick strip 5½" wide and the background strips 4" wide. Make the crosscuts 3½" wide.

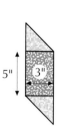

Finished Brick Dimensions

VARIATIONS

For a scrappy border, make shorter strip units using many fabrics, then arrange the crosscuts randomly. You could also arrange the bricks in a repeating design, such as alternating two fabrics.

Scrappy Bricks

Repeating Bricks

Altering the length and width of the bricks will change the appearance of the border. This is what the border looks like using the same strip unit but making the crosscuts only 1½" wide.

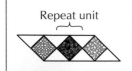

Repeat unit

Finished border width: 2.12"

Finished size of repeat unit: 2.12"

Squares on Point

This is one of my favorite pieced borders. It's simple to make and to plan, it's not a challenge to change the size, and the corner squares are easy to add. The border looks good either in one fabric, a planned series of fabrics, or completely scrappy. Squares on Point also makes nice sashing strips between the blocks of a quilt. If you use the same background fabric for your blocks and the border, as in "Puss in Bonnets" (page 14), all you see are the rows of squares.

PLANNING YOUR BORDER

Each strip unit will make about 44" of border. Estimate the amount of fabric you need from the examples below.

Quilt Size	Total Length of Borders	No. of Strip Units	Squares Fabric	Background Fabric
Wall quilt (30" x 45")	150"	4	⅓ yd.	⅔ yd.
Bed quilt (90" x 110")	400"	9½	⅔ yd.	1⅓ yds.

CUTTING AND ASSEMBLY

See "Speed Piecing" on pages 25–26.

1. Cut strips the widths shown in the diagram and construct a strip unit. Press the seam allowances as indicated. Make 2"-wide crosscuts.

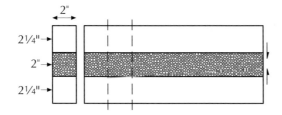

2. Join pairs of crosscuts, right sides together, offsetting the crosscuts and matching the seams as shown.

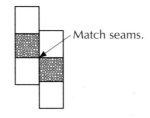

Match seams.

3. Sew the pairs together into fours, the fours into eights, and so on. Press the seam allowances in one direction, pressing carefully to avoid distorting the bias edges.

4. Trim the long edges, leaving a ¼"-wide seam allowance.

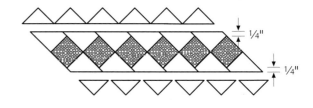

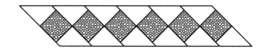

CORNERS

Each border strip must begin and end with a whole square. The finished length of each side of the quilt top before the pieced border is added must be equal to a number of complete repeats of the squares on point. For example:

10 repeats x 2.12" each = 21.2"
22 repeats x 2.12" each = 46.6"

Round the length of the borders to the nearest ⅛" or ¼", and add coping strips to bring the quilt top up to the desired measurements. (See "Making a Border That Fits" on pages 7–11.)

1. Square off each end of the side border strips by adding a background triangle and trimming as shown. To make the triangles, cut a 2¾" square in half twice diagonally. Sew the side borders to the quilt top.

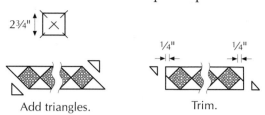

Add triangles.   Trim.

2. For the corners, add 1 more crosscut to each end of the top and bottom borders. Referring to step 1, square the ends of the top and bottom borders, then sew them to the quilt top.

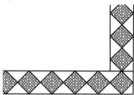

CHANGING THE SIZE

To make borders of smaller or larger squares, refer to the chart below.

Border Width* Strip Width	Squares Strip Width	Background Width	Crosscuts
1.41"	1½"	1¾"	1½"
1.77"	1¾"	2"	1¾"
2.12"	2"	2¼"	2"
2.47"	2¼"	2½"	2¼"
2.83"	2½"	2¾"	2½"

*The border width equals the width of the repeat unit.

VARIATIONS

For a scrappy border, make shorter strip units using many fabrics, then arrange the crosscuts randomly.

The squares can also be arranged in a repeating design, or shaded from dark to light and back to dark again.

Repeat Design

Dark to Light to Dark

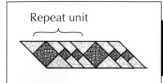

Repeat unit

Finished
border
width:
4.24"

Finished
size of
repeat
unit:
8.48"

Beads on a String

This is a simple variation of Squares on Point. It's especially effective on large quilts.

PLANNING YOUR BORDER

Each set of strip units will make about 84" of border. Estimate the amount of fabric you need from the examples below.

Quilt Size	Total Length of Borders	No. of Strip Unit Sets	Bead Fabric	Background Fabric
Wall quilt (30" x 45")	150"	2	½ yd.	1¼ yds.
Bed quilt (90" x 110")	400"	5	1 yd.	2⅓ yds.

CUTTING AND ASSEMBLY

See "Speed Piecing" on pages 25–26.

1. Construct strip units A and B, cutting the strips the widths shown in the diagram. Press the seam allowances as indicated. Make 2"-wide crosscuts from strip unit A, and 3½"-wide crosscuts from strip unit B.

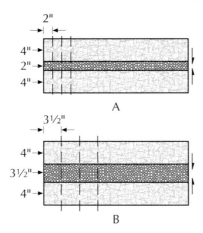

A

B

2. Join pairs of BA, AB, and AA crosscuts, right sides together, offsetting the crosscuts and matching the seams as shown.

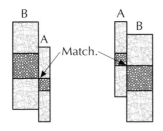

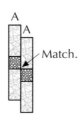

3. Sew the pairs into fours, and the fours into eights, continuing until the borders are long enough for the quilt top. As you sew the pairs together, maintain the pattern of 1 large square, 2 small squares, 1 large, 2 small, and so on. Press all seam allowances in one direction.

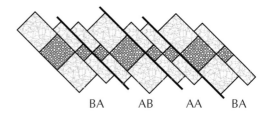

BA   AB   AA   BA

4. Trim the long edges, leaving a ¼"-wide seam allowance.

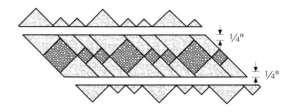

¼"

¼"

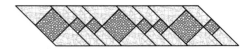

CORNERS

Each border strip must begin and end with two small squares. The finished length of each side of the quilt top before the Beads on a String border is added must be equal to a number of complete units plus two small squares (2 x 2.12"). For example:

10 repeats x 8.48" each = 84.8" + 4.24" = 89"
13 repeats x 8.48" each = 110.2" + 4.24" = 114.4"

Round the lengths of the borders to the nearest 1⁄8" or 1⁄4", and add coping strips to bring the quilt top up to the desired measurements. (See "Making a Border That Fits" on pages 7–11.)

1. Assemble the top and bottom borders.
2. Cut 4 squares of background fabric, each 3⁷⁄8" x 3⁷⁄8", in half once diagonally. Add 1 triangle to each end of each border to square off the end.

3⁷⁄8"

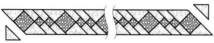

Add triangles.

3. Trim the ends of each border as shown, leaving a 1⁄4"-wide seam allowance.

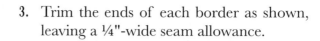

1⁄4"   1⁄4"

4. Sew the top and bottom borders to the quilt top.
5. Assemble the side borders, then add a B crosscut to each end of the borders for the corners. Square the ends as in steps 2 and 3.
6. Sew the side borders to the quilt top.

CHANGING THE SIZE

To make a smaller or larger border design, cut strips, referring to the dimensions in the chart below.

Border Width	Repeat Unit	STRIP WIDTH					
		Bead A	Background A	Crosscut A	Bead B	Background B	Crosscut B
2.82"	5.64"	1½"	3"	1½"	2½"	3"	2½"
3.54"	7.08"	1¾"	3½"	1¾"	3"	3½"	3"
4.24"	8.48"	2"	4"	2"	3½"	4"	3½"
4.95"	9.90"	2¼"	4½"	2¼"	4"	4½"	4"
5.66"	11.32"	2½"	5"	2½"	4½"	5"	4½"

VARIATIONS

For a scrappy border, make several strip units from several different bead fabrics, then arrange the crosscuts randomly.

Scrappy Border

You can create a repeating design by using one fabric for the small beads and a different fabric for the large beads.

Repeat Border

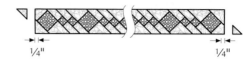

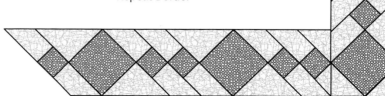

Repeat unit
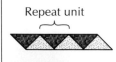

Small Dogtooth

Finished border width: 1.41"

Finished size of repeat unit: 2.83"

This speed-pieced border won't overwhelm your quilt, and it combines well with other pieced borders. For tiny Dogtooth borders, use the foundation-piecing patterns on page 92.

PLANNING YOUR BORDER

Each strip unit will make about 45" of border. Estimate the amount of fabric you need from the examples below.

Quilt Size	Total Length of Borders	No. of Strip Units	Dogtooth Fabric	Background Fabric
Wall quilt (30" x 45")	150"	3½	⅓ yd.	⅓ yd.
Bed quilt (90" x 110")	400"	9	1 yd.	1 yd.

CUTTING AND ASSEMBLY

See "Speed Piecing" on pages 25–26.

1. Construct a strip unit, cutting the strips the width shown in the diagram. Press the seam allowance as indicated. Before making crosscuts, draw a line on the wrong side of the dogtooth fabric ½" from the top edge of the strip unit (2" from the seam line). Make 2½"-wide crosscuts.

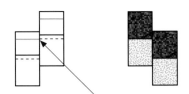

Draw line on back of unit.

2. Join the crosscuts in pairs, matching the drawn line on one crosscut with the seam of the other crosscut.

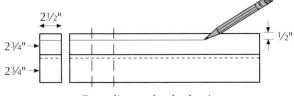

Match seam with line drawn on wrong side.

3. Sew the pairs into fours, and the fours into eights, matching the drawn line to the seam each time and continuing until the borders are long enough for the quilt top.

4. Press all seam allowances in one direction, being careful not to stretch the border strip. Trim the long edges, leaving a ¼"-wide seam allowance.

CORNERS

Each border strip must begin and end with a whole dogtooth. The finished length of each side of the quilt top before the Dogtooth border is added must be equal to a number of complete repeats. For example:

10 repeats x 2.83" each = 28.3"
22 repeats x 2.83" each = 62.3"

Adjust the length of each border to the nearest ⅛" or ¼", and add coping strips to bring the quilt top up to the desired measurements. (See "Making a Border That Fits" on pages 7–11.)

1. Trim the ends of the borders, leaving a ¼"-wide seam allowance.

Trim.

2. Sew the side borders to the quilt top.
3. Cut 4 background corner squares, each

2" x 2". Sew the squares to the ends of the top and bottom borders.

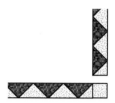

Add corner squares.

4. Sew the top and bottom borders to the quilt top, then trim the edges of the corners even with the borders.

For a different corner, see the "Large Dogtooth" border on page 63.

CHANGING THE SIZE

To make smaller or larger Dogtooth borders, refer to the chart below.

Border Width	Repeat Unit	Dogtooth Strip	Background Strip	Crosscut Width
0.88"	1.76"	2"	2"	1¾"
1.06"	2.12"	2¼"	2¼"	2"
1.24"	2.47"	2½"	2½"	2¼"
1.41"	2.83"	2¾"	2¾"	2½"
1.59"	3.18"	3"	3"	2¾"
1.77"	3.54"	3¼"	3¼"	3"
1.94"	3.89"	3½"	3½"	3¼"

VARIATIONS

Make a number of strip units from different dogtooth fabrics and mix the crosscuts for a scrappy border.

Scrappy Border

Make a Double Dogtooth border by sewing together two border strips for each side of the quilt. Match the dogtooth units or offset them.

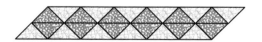

Matched Dogtooth Units

Offset Dogtooth Units

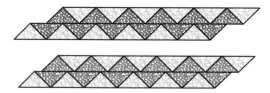

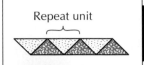

Repeat unit

Finished border width: 2"

Finished size of repeat unit: 4"

Large Dogtooth

Although it looks just like the Small Dogtooth border, this one is constructed differently. The method used here is better for larger triangles. It's also a good one to use for a scrappy border, as the rectangles can be cut from small scraps of different fabrics.

PLANNING YOUR BORDER

Each ¼ yard of fabric will make about 27 rectangles. Estimate the amount of fabric you need from the examples below.

Quilt Size	Total Length of Borders	No. of Dogtooth Rectangles	Dogtooth Fabric	Background Fabric
Wall quilt (30" x 45")	150"	40*	½ yd.	½ yd.
Bed quilt (90" x 110")	400"	102*	1 yd.	1 yd.

*Cut an equal number of background rectangles.

CUTTING AND ASSEMBLY

See "Speed-Pieced Corners" on pages 25–26.

1. Cut the number of 2½" x 4½" dogtooth and background fabric rectangles required for your quilt.

2. Speed-piece background rectangles to dogtooth rectangles as shown.

Stitch.   Trim.   Press.

3. Speed-piece the pairs as shown. Sew the pairs into fours, and the fours into eights, continuing until the borders are long enough for the quilt top. Begin and end each border strip with a background rectangle.

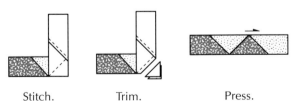

Stitch.   Trim.   Press.

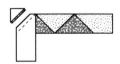 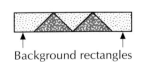

Background rectangles

4. Trim the long edges and the ends of the border, leaving a ¼"-wide seam allowance.

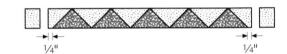

¼"   ¼"

CORNERS

Follow steps 1–5 for the "Small Dogtooth" corners on page 61, but cut the background corner squares 2½" x 2½".

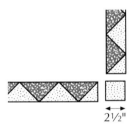 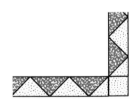

2½"

Add corner square.

For a different corner, the length of each border must still be a number of complete repeat units, but begin and end each border with a half unit. For example, if the length of the border is 12 dogtooth units, sew a border starting with half of a dogtooth unit, add 11 complete units, and end with another half unit. The easiest way to do this is to make the border 13 complete units long, then trim half of a unit off each end, leaving a ¼"-wide seam allowance. Construct the side borders in this manner.

The top and bottom borders must also begin and end with half units. On these border strips, however, don't trim off the excess half units; they take the place of the corner squares.

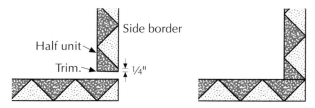

CHANGING THE SIZE

The rectangles can be any size, as long as the finished length is twice the finished width.

VARIATIONS

See "Small Dogtooth" variations on page 61.

Repeat unit

Folded Ribbon

Finished
border
width:
2.12"

Finished
size of
repeat
unit:
4.24"

This speed-pieced border looks like a continuous piece of ribbon, folded so you see first the upper side and then the lower side, all the way around the quilt. The upper side of the ribbon runs across two corners, and the underside of the ribbon runs across the other two corners. To maintain the folded illusion, select two similar fabrics for the ribbon, one a little darker than the other.

PLANNING YOUR BORDER

Each strip unit will make about 67" of border. You can make approximately 16 crosscuts from each strip unit, so you will need 16 of the 1½" x 5" rectangles of light ribbon fabric for each strip unit. Estimate the amount of fabric you need from the examples below.

Quilt Size	Total Length of Borders	No. of Strip Units	Dark Ribbon Fabric	Light Ribbon Fabric	Background Fabric
Wall quilt (30" x 45")	150"	2½	¼ yd.	¼ yd.	½ yd.
Bed quilt (90" x 110")	400"	6½	⅓ yd.	⅔ yd.	1¼ yds.

CUTTING AND ASSEMBLY

See "Speed Piecing" on pages 25–26.

1. Construct a strip unit from the background fabric and the dark ribbon fabric, cutting the strips the widths shown in the diagram. Press seam allowances toward the ribbon.

2. On the wrong side of the strip units, draw a line ½" above the top seam and ½" below the bottom seam on the background fabric.

3. Make 2½"-wide crosscuts.

4. Cut the light ribbon fabric into 1½" x 5" rectangles, one for each crosscut.

5. Sew the light ribbon fabric rectangles to the crosscuts, lining up the end of each light strip with the drawn line on the crosscut. For 2 of the borders, stagger the pieces *down*; for the remaining borders, stagger the pieces *up*. Press the seam allowances toward the light ribbon rectangles, away from the crosscuts.

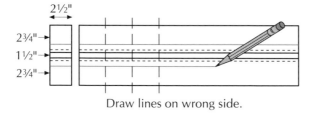

2½"

2¾"
1½"
2¾"

Draw lines on wrong side.

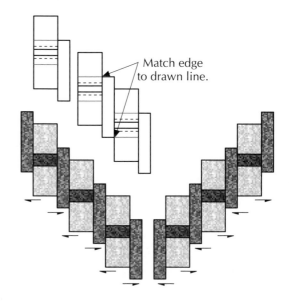

Match edge to drawn line.

6. Trim the long edges, leaving a ¼"-wide seam allowance.

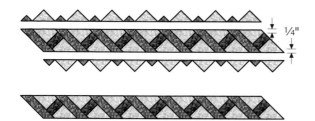

CORNERS

Each border strip begins and ends with a crosscut. The finished length of each side of the quilt top before the Folded Ribbon border is added must be equal to a number of complete repeats plus the width of one crosscut (3.54"). For example:

10 repeats x 4.24" each = 42.4" + 3.54" = 45.9"
22 repeats x 4.24" each = 93.3" + 3.54" = 96.8"

Round the lengths of the borders to the nearest ⅛" or ¼", and add coping strips to bring the quilt top up to the desired measurements. (See "Making a Border That Fits" on pages 7–11.)

1. Sew the borders to the four sides of the quilt top, starting and stopping ¼" from the corners.
2. Two of the corners are simple miters. (See "Corners" on pages 10–11.)
3. For each of the remaining corners, add a 1½" x 7" rectangle of the light ribbon fabric. For the corner triangles, cut 4" squares of background fabric in half diagonally.
4. Center, then sew the corners to the quilt. Trim the light ribbon rectangles and the background corners even with the outer edges of the borders.

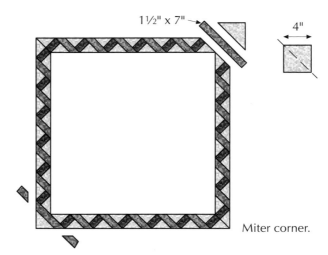

1½" x 7"

4"

Miter corner.

CHANGING THE SIZE

The directions above are for a ribbon with a finished width of 1". If you want your ribbon to be wider or narrower, follow the chart below.

Finished Width of Ribbon	Border Width	Repeat Unit	Dark Ribbon Strips	Background Strips	Crosscut Width	Light Ribbon Pieces
¾"	1.59"	3.18"	1¼" x 42"	2¼" x 42"	2"	1¼" x 4"
1"	2.12"	4.24"	1½" x 42"	2¾" x 42"	2½"	1½" x 5"
1¼"	2.65"	5.30"	1¾" x 42"	3¼" x 42"	3"	1¾" x 6"
1½"	3.18"	6.36"	2" x 42"	3¾" x 42"	3½"	2" x 7"
1¾"	3.71"	7.42"	2¼" x 42"	4¼" x 42"	4"	2¼" x 8"
2"	4.24"	8.48"	2½" x 42"	4¾" x 42"	4½"	2½" x 9"

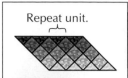

Repeat unit.

Finished border width: 2.82"

Finished size of repeat unit: 1.41"

Shaded Squares

The success of this border depends on careful fabric selection. You need a smooth transition
from light to dark, starting with your quilt's background fabric.

PLANNING YOUR BORDER

One five-fabric strip unit will make about 40" of border; the four corners require an additional strip unit. Estimate the amount of fabric you need from the examples below.

Quilt Size	Total Length of Borders	No. of Strip Units	Fabric 1*	Fabric 2	Fabric 3	Fabric 4	Fabric 5**
Wall quilt (30" x 45")	150"	5	⅓ yd.	¼ yd.	¼ yd.	¼ yd.	⅓ yd.
Bed quilt (90" x 110")	400"	11	⅔ yd.	½ yd.	½ yd.	½ yd.	⅔ yd.

*Use background fabric for Fabric 1.
**You may wish to purchase additional Fabric 5 for binding.

CUTTING AND ASSEMBLY

See "Speed Piecing" on pages 25–26.

1. Construct a strip unit from the border fabrics, cutting the strips the widths shown in the diagram. Arrange and sew the strips in gradated order. Use the background fabric from your quilt for the strip that will be sewn next to the quilt top. For half of the strip units, press the seam allowances toward the darker fabrics. For the remaining strip units, press the seam allowances toward the lighter fabrics. If your quilt requires an odd number of strip units, cut 1 of the strip units in half before pressing.

2. Make 1½"-wide crosscuts.

1½"

1¾" →
1½" →
1½" →
1½" →
1¾" →

Background Fabric

3. Alternate the crosscuts pressed in one direction with the crosscuts pressed in the opposite direction. Sew the crosscuts together, offsetting as shown, matching seams and butting seam allowances against each other. Press the seam allowances in one direction, pressing carefully to avoid distorting the bias edges.

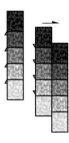

4. Trim the long edges, leaving a ¼"-wide seam allowance.

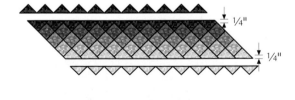

¼"

¼"

CORNERS

Each border strip must begin and end with a whole crosscut. The finished length of each side of the quilt top before the Shaded Squares border is added must be equal to a number of complete repeats. For example:

10 repeats x 1.41" each = 14.1"
22 repeats x 1.41" each = 31.0"

Round the lengths of the borders to the nearest ⅛" or ¼", and add coping strips to bring the quilt top up to the desired measurements. (See "Making a Border That Fits" on pages 7–11.)

1. For each corner, make a triangle unit from crosscuts, removing, discarding, and trimming squares as shown.
2. Sew a triangle to the right end of each border.
3. Sew the borders to the 4 sides of the quilt top, starting and stopping ¼" from the corners.
4. Miter the corners. (See "Corners" on pages 10–11.)

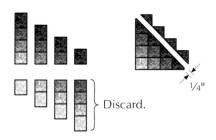

Discard.

1/4"

With a little more effort, you can make corners that continue the shaded design. Each border is still a number of complete repeats, but each begins and ends with a half repeat, and the right end of each border extends one-half of a repeat past the corner of the quilt top. Calculate the number of crosscuts needed for each border as you did at left, then add one crosscut to each border strip.

1. Prepare 4 borders, following steps 1–3 of "Cutting and Assembly" on page 66. Before sewing the first 4 crosscuts together, remove squares from each border as shown.

Discard.

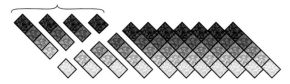

2. Trim the long edges, leaving a ¼"-wide seam allowance.

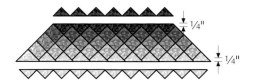

1/4"
1/4"

3. Square up the left end of each border as shown, leaving a ¼"-wide seam allowance.

1/4"

4. Sew the top border to the quilt top, starting with the left edge and stopping 2" short of the right edge.

Top border   Stop stitching here.

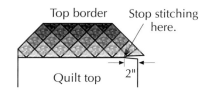

Quilt top   2"

5. Sew the left border to the quilt top, then the bottom border, then the right border. Now sew the open 2" of the top border to the quilt top.

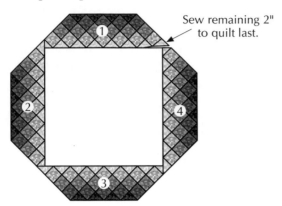

Sew remaining 2" to quilt last.

6. For each corner, make a pieced triangle unit from crosscuts, removing and discarding squares as shown. Sew a pieced triangle unit to each corner of the quilt.

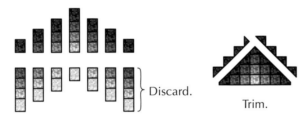

Discard.

Trim.

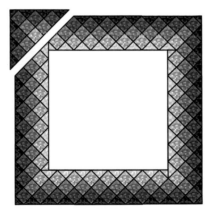

CHANGING THE SIZE

The strips can be cut any width. Cut the first and last strips ¼" wider than the others. The crosscut width is equal to the cut width of the inner strips.

VARIATIONS

Instead of shading from light to dark, you can make a striped border. In the strip unit, alternate strips of contrasting fabrics with strips of background fabric.

Striped Border

Or, use a number of fabrics to make the border scrappy.

Scrappy Border

Arrows

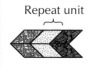
Repeat unit

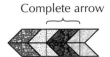
Complete arrow

The appearance of this adaptable speed-pieced border changes with your fabric selection. It is made from two long pieced strips sewn side by side. You can change its appearance either by matching the two strips, making arrow shapes, or staggering them so they look like leaves on a vine. Smaller versions of this border can be foundation-pieced, using the patterns on page 94.

Finished border width: 3"

Finished size of repeat unit: 2.12" (complete arrow is 3.62")

PLANNING YOUR BORDER

Each set of strip units will make about 160" of border. Estimate the amount of fabric you need from the examples below.

Quilt Size	Total Length of Borders	No. of Strip Unit Sets	Arrow Fabric	Background Fabric
Wall quilt (30" x 45)	150"	1	⅓ yd.	⅓ yd.
Bed quilt (90" x 110")	400"	3	¾ yd.	¾ yd.

CUTTING AND ASSEMBLY

See "Speed Piecing" on pages 25–26.

1. Construct 2 mirror-image strip units, cutting all the strips 2" wide. Stair-step each strip unit, adding each new strip 1½" from the end of the previous strip as shown. Press the seam allowances of the 2 strip units in opposite directions.

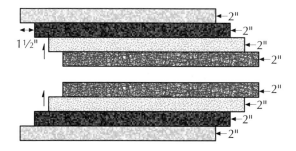

2. Trim 1 end of each strip unit at a 45° angle.

3. Make 2"-wide crosscuts, maintaining the 45° angle. The crosscuts from each strip unit should be mirror images of each other.

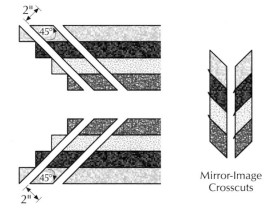

Mirror-Image Crosscuts

4. Join pairs of crosscuts cut from the same strip unit, end to end. Press the new seam allowances in the same direction as those in the strip unit.

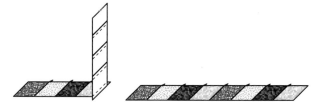

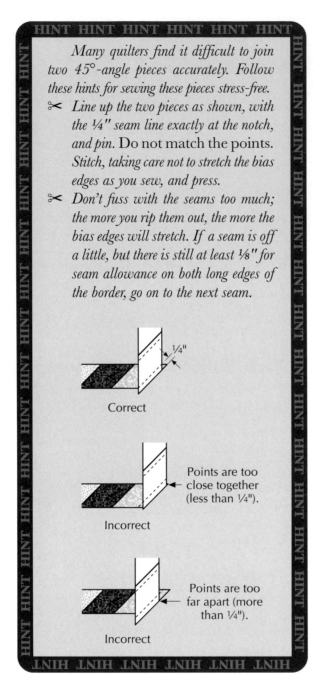

Many quilters find it difficult to join two 45°-angle pieces accurately. Follow these hints for sewing these pieces stress-free.

✄ *Line up the two pieces as shown, with the ¼" seam line exactly at the notch, and pin. Do not match the points. Stitch, taking care not to stretch the bias edges as you sew, and press.*

✄ *Don't fuss with the seams too much; the more you rip them out, the more the bias edges will stretch. If a seam is off a little, but there is still at least ⅛" for seam allowance on both long edges of the border, go on to the next seam.*

¼"

Correct

Points are too close together (less than ¼").

Incorrect

Points are too far apart (more than ¼").

Incorrect

5.   Sew the pairs into fours, and the fours into eights, continuing until the strips are long enough for the quilt top.

6.   Repeat steps 4 and 5 with crosscuts from the mirror-image strip unit.

7.   Before joining the long mirror-image strips, review "Corners" at right. After preparing the ends of the strips as instructed, sew the 2 long strips together, matching the fabrics and seams to form arrows.

CORNERS

The arrows reverse direction in the middle of each border and touch points in all four corners. Each half border, from the center to the corner of the completed Arrows border, must include a number of complete arrows. The finished length of each side of the quilt top before the border is added must be equal to a number of complete repeats. For example:

10 repeats x 2.12" each = 21.2"
22 repeats x 2.12" each = 46.6"

Round the lengths of the borders to the nearest ⅛" or ¼", and add coping strips to bring the quilt top up to the desired measurements. (See "Making a Border That Fits" on pages 7–11.)

1.   Square the end of each long strip by adding background triangles. To make the triangles, cut 2⅜" squares in half once diagonally.

2⅜"

Add triangles.

2.   Sew the long strips together to make the arrows, with seam allowances pressed in opposite directions and butting against each other at each seam.

3. Sew the 2 halves of each border together.

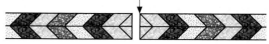

Border center

4. Sew the borders to all 4 sides of the quilt top, starting and stopping ¼" from each corner of the quilt top.

5. Miter the corners. (See "Corners" on pages 10–11.)

6. Cut 2 background squares, each 3⅞" x 3⅞", in half diagonally; add to the corners.

3⅞"

Add corner triangle.

CHANGING THE SIZE

It is easy to make this border smaller or larger; all the strips for the strip units are cut the same width. The finished width of this border is always twice the finished width of the strips. The repeat unit is 1.414 times the finished width of the strips; the length of a whole arrow is the repeat unit plus the finished width of one strip. For example:

Cut Width of Strips	Border Width	Repeat Unit	Whole Arrow
1½"	2"	1.41"	2.41"
2"	3"	2.12"	3.62"
2½"	4"	2.82"	4.82"

VARIATIONS

Alternate one arrow fabric with the background fabric.

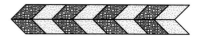

For arrows in two alternating colors, alternate two arrow fabrics with the background fabric.

Select 4 (or more) fabrics in a gradated sequence to make shaded arrows.

At step 7 of "Cutting and Assembly," as you sew the two long strips of crosscuts together, offset the arrow and background fabrics to make "leaves" instead of arrows.

At step 4 of "Cutting and Assembly," make a border from just one of the two long strips of diamonds.

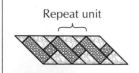
Repeat unit

Finished border width: 3.54"

Finished size of repeat unit: 3.54"

Zigzag

This is the border to use when you want to make a bold statement.

PLANNING YOUR BORDER

Each set of strip units will make about 85" of border. Estimate the amount of fabric you need from the examples below.

Quilt Size	Total Length of Borders	No. of Strip Unit Sets	Zigzag Fabric	Background Fabric
Wall quilt (30" x 45")	150"	2	½ yd.	¾ yd.
Bed quilt (90" x 110")	400"	5	1 yd.	1¾ yds.

CUTTING AND ASSEMBLY

See "Speed Piecing" on pages 25–26.

1. Construct strip units A and B, cutting the strips the widths shown in the diagram. Press the seam allowances as indicated; this is especially important with this border.
2. Make 1¾"-wide crosscuts.

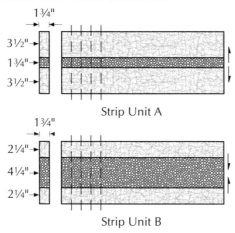

1¾"

3½" →
1¾" →
3½" →

Strip Unit A

1¾"

2¼" →
4¼" →
2¼" →

Strip Unit B

3. Join a crosscut from each strip unit in pairs, matching the seams as shown.

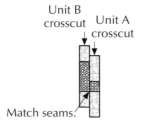

Unit B crosscut   Unit A crosscut

Match seams.

4. Sew the pairs into fours, and the fours into eights, continuing until the borders are long enough for the quilt top.

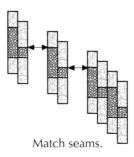

Match seams.

5. When the border strip is complete, press all seam allowances in one direction. Press carefully to avoid distorting the bias edges.
6. Trim the long edges, leaving a ¼"-wide seam allowance.

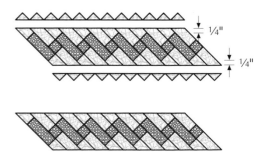

¼"

¼"

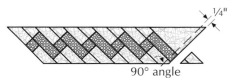

CORNERS

Each border strip must begin with an A crosscut and end with a B crosscut. The finished length of each side of the quilt top before the Zigzag border is added must be equal to a number of complete repeats. (Each pair of crosscuts is a repeat unit.) For example:

10 repeats x 3.54" each = 35.4"
22 repeats x 3.54" each = 77.9"

Round the lengths of the borders to the nearest ⅛" or ¼", and add coping strips to bring the quilt top up to the desired measurements. (See "Making a Border That Fits" on pages 7–11.)

1. Construct each border with 2 additional crosscuts at the right end.
2. Cut 1 square, 5" x 5", from background fabric, then cut it in half twice diagonally. Sew the short edge of a triangle to the right end of each border as shown.

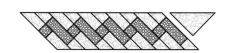

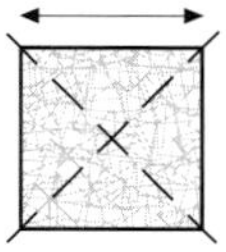

3. Trim the right end of each border even with the background triangle.

4. Sew the borders to all 4 sides of the quilt top, starting and stopping ¼" from the corners.
5. Miter the corners. (See "Corners" on pages 10–11.)

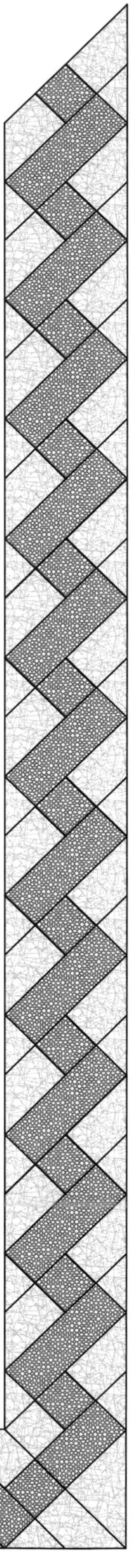

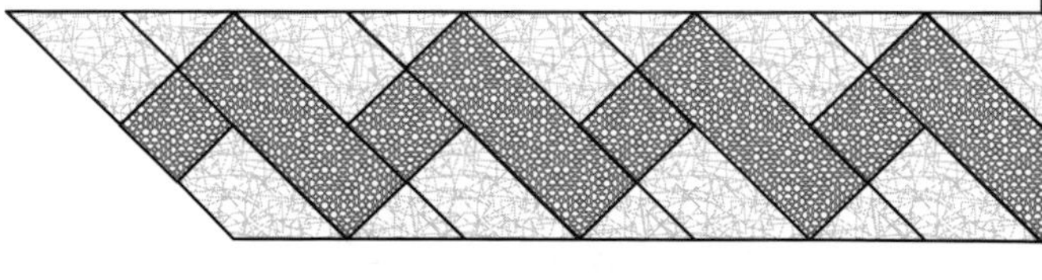

CHANGING THE SIZE

Follow the chart below to prepare strip units for smaller and larger Zigzag designs. "Zigzag Size" refers to the finished width of the Zigzag fabric. (The directions given above are for a 1¼"-wide Zigzag.) The measurements in the chart below are the cut widths of the strips for strip units A and B.

Zigzag Size	Border Width (= Repeat Unit)	Zigzag A	Background A	Zigzag B	Background B
¾"	2.12"	1¼"	2¼"	2¾"	1½"
1"	2.82"	1½"	3"	3½"	2"
1¼"	3.54"	1¾"	3½"	4¼"	2¼"
1½"	4.24"	2"	4"	5"	2½"
1¾"	4.95"	2¼"	4½"	5¾"	2¾"
2"	5.66"	2½"	5"	6½"	3"

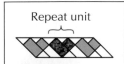

Repeat unit

Finished border width: 2.48"

Finished size of repeat unit: 3.19"

Side-by-Side Hearts

This cheerful speed-pieced border is presented in two sizes, one for wall hangings and one for bed-size quilts.

PLANNING YOUR BORDER

Each set of strip units will make about 76" of border. Estimate the amount of fabric you need from the examples below.

SMALL HEART BORDER

Quilt Size	Total Length of Borders	No. of Strip Unit Sets	Heart Fabric	Background Fabric
Wall quilt (30" x 45")	150"	2	⅓ yd.	⅔ yd.
Bed quilt (90" x 110")	400"	5½	1 yd.	1⅔ yds.

CUTTING AND ASSEMBLY

See "Speed Piecing" on pages 25–26.

1. Construct strip units A and B, cutting the strips the widths shown in the diagram. Press the seam allowances as indicated.

2. Make 1½"-wide crosscuts in strip unit A, and 1¾"-wide crosscuts in strip unit B.

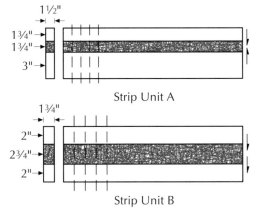

Strip Unit A

Strip Unit B

3. Join pairs of crosscuts, one crosscut from each strip unit, matching the seams as shown.

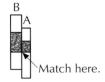

B
A
Match here.

4. Sew the pairs into fours, and the fours into eights, continuing until the borders are long enough for the quilt top. Press the seam allowances in one direction, pressing carefully to avoid distorting the bias edges.

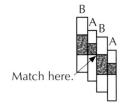

B
A
B
A
Match here.

5. Trim the long edges, leaving a ¼"-wide seam allowance.

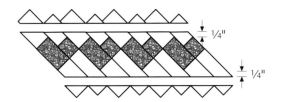

¼"

¼"

CORNERS

Each border strip must begin and end with a whole heart. The finished length of each side of the quilt before the Side-by-Side Hearts border is added must be equal to a number of complete hearts. For example:

10 repeats x 3.19" each = 31.9"
22 repeats x 3.19" each = 70.2"

Round the lengths of each border to the nearest ⅛" or ¼", and add coping strips to bring the quilt top up to the desired measurements. (See "Making a Border That Fits" on pages 7–11.)

1. Add 1 large triangle to the left end of each border, and 1 small triangle to the right end. To make the large triangles, cut 2 squares, each 2½" x 2½", and for the small triangles, cut 2 squares, each 1¾" x 1¾", from background fabric. Cut each square in half once diagonally.

Add large triangle.   Add small triangle.

2. Trim the ends of the borders, leaving a ¼"-wide seam allowance.

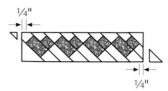

3. From the background fabric, cut 4 squares, each 3" x 3", for the corner squares. Sew the squares to the side border strips and trim the squares even with the long edges of the border. Sew the top and bottom borders to the quilt, then the side borders. Trim.

CHANGING THE SIZE

The directions make hearts in a good size for a wall hanging. For a larger, 4.95"-wide border (more suitable for a bed-size quilt), cut strips in the following widths. The repeat unit is 6.36".

	Heart Fabric	Background	Crosscuts
Strip Unit A	3"	3"	2½"
		5½"	
Strip Unit B	5"	3½"	3"

Each pair of strip units will make about 90" of border. Estimate the amount of fabric you need from the example below.

LARGE HEART BORDER

Quilt Size	Total Length of Borders	No. of Strip Unit Sets	Heart Fabric	Background Fabric
Bed quilt (90" x 110")	400"	5	1⅓ yds.	2⅓ yds.

VARIATIONS

Make two sets of strip units, using two different heart fabrics, and alternate the hearts made from each fabric. Or, for a scrappy border, make a number of sets of shorter strip units from a variety of heart fabrics.

Alternate Fabric Hearts   Scrappy Hearts

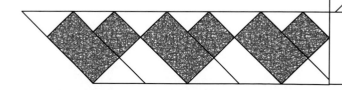

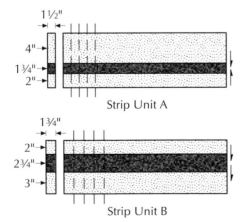

Finished border width: 3.19"

Finished size of repeat: 3.19"

Vertical Hearts

Use this version of the hearts border by itself, or combine it with "Side-by-Side Hearts" (page 74) to make a border in which all the hearts are right side up.

PLANNING YOUR BORDER

Each set of strip units will make about 76" of border. Estimate the amount of fabric you need from the examples below.

SMALL HEART BORDER

Quilt Size	Total Length of Borders	No. of Strip Unit Sets	Heart Fabric	Background Fabric
Wall quilt (30" x 45")	150"	2	⅓ yd.	¾ yd.
Bed quilt (90" x 110")	400"	5½	1 yd.	2 yds.

CUTTING AND ASSEMBLY

See "Speed Piecing" on pages 25–26.

1. Construct strip units A and B, cutting the strips the widths shown in the diagrams below. Press the seam allowances as indicated. On the wrong side of strip unit A, draw a line 1" from the seam on the wide background strip.

1"

Draw a line on the wrong side of strip unit A.

2. Make 1½"-wide crosscuts in strip unit A, and 1¾"-wide crosscuts in strip unit B.

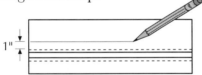

1½"

4"

1¾"

2"

Strip Unit A

1¾"

2"

2¾"

3"

Strip Unit B

3. Join 1 crosscut from each strip unit in pairs, matching the seams as shown.

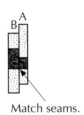

B A

Match seams.

4. Sew the pairs into fours, matching the seam lines to the drawn lines as shown. Sew the fours into eights, continuing until the borders are long enough for the quilt top. Press the seam allowances in one direction, pressing carefully to avoid distorting the bias edges.

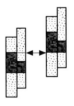

Match seams with line drawn on wrong side.

5. Trim the long edges, leaving a ¼"-wide seam allowance.

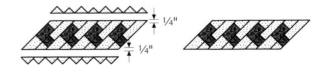

¼"

¼"

CORNERS

Each border strip must begin and end with an entire heart repeat. The finished length of each side of the quilt before the Vertical Hearts border is added must be equal to a number of complete heart repeats. For example:

10 repeats x 3.19" each = 31.9"
22 repeats x 3.19" each = 70.2"

Round the lengths of the borders to the nearest ⅛" or ¼", and add coping strips to bring the quilt top up to the desired measurements. (See "Making a Border That Fits" on pages 7–11.)

Finish the hearts at both ends of the side borders.

1. From the background fabric, cut 2 squares, each 2½" x 2½", and 2 squares, each 1¾" x 1¾". Cut each square in half once diagonally. Add 1 large background triangle to the left end of each border, and 1 small triangle to the right end. Trim the triangles even with the edges of the border strips.

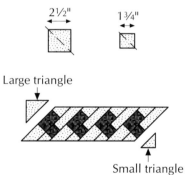

2. Trim the ends of the borders as shown, leaving a ¼"-wide seam allowance.

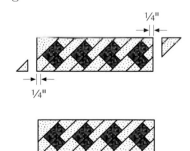

3. Cut 4 background squares, each 3¾" x 3¾", for the corners. Sew to the border strips and trim the squares even with the edges of the border.

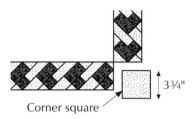

Corner square

If you would like the hearts to be right side up all around your quilt, you can make the top and bottom borders from "Side-by-Side Hearts," and the side borders from "Vertical Hearts." The top and bottom borders should begin and end with an entire heart. Extend each end of the top and bottom borders by one heart for the corners. The side borders, including the corners, should be a number of complete hearts, as shown in the diagram below.

A little extra calculation is necessary, however. Notice that there is a little spacer distance above each vertical heart and that the spacer is trimmed at the top of each of the side borders. For the side borders with the extra hearts at the top and bottom to fit, the sides of the quilt top before adding borders must be equal in length to a number of complete repeats *plus* about ¾". One way to think of this is that the side of the quilt top must be long enough for a number of heart repeats plus the spacer for the heart on the bottom corner.

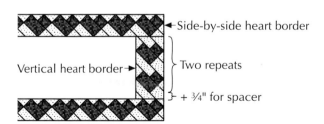

Side-by-side heart border

Vertical heart border

Two repeats

+ ¾" for spacer

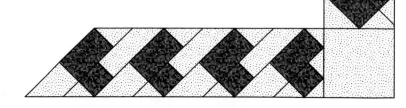

CHANGING THE SIZE

The directions make a border in a good size for a wall hanging. For a larger, 6.36"-wide border (more suitable for a bed-size quilt), cut strips in the following widths. The repeat unit is 6.36".

	Heart Fabric	Background	Crosscuts
Strip Unit A	3"	3"	2½"
		7½"	
Strip Unit B	5"	3½"	3"
		5½"	

Each set of strip units will make about 90" of border. Estimate the amount of fabric you need from the example below.

LARGE HEART BORDER

Quilt Size	Total Length of Borders	No. of Strip Unit Sets	Heart Fabric	Background Fabric
Bed quilt (90" x 110")	400"	5	1⅓ yds.	3 yds.

Twined Border

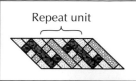

Repeat unit

Two intertwined lines zigzag around the quilt in this striking speed-pieced border. The strip units must be sewn carefully and accurately, but after that, the border and corners go together quickly. Make sure the two intertwined fabrics contrast clearly with each other and with the background.

Finished border width: 4.24"

Finished size of repeat unit: 5.66"

PLANNING YOUR BORDER

Since a repeat unit is made of 1 crosscut from strip unit A, 1 from B, and 2 from C, a set of strip units for this border includes 1 strip unit A, 1 strip unit B, and 2 strip units C. Each set of strip units will make about 158" of border. You will need additional crosscuts for the corners. Estimate the amount of fabric you need from the examples below.

Quilt Size	Total Length of Borders	No. of Strip Unit Sets	Fabric A	Fabric B	Background Fabric
Wall quilt (30" x 45")	150"	1	⅓ yd.	⅓ yd.	¾ yd.
Bed quilt (90" x 110")	400"	3	⅔ yd.	⅔ yd.	2 yds.

CUTTING AND ASSEMBLY

See "Speed Piecing" on pages 25–26.

1. Construct strip units A, B, and C, cutting the strips the widths shown in the diagrams.

1¾"→
5½"→
1¾"→

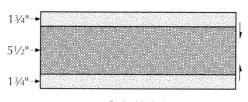

Strip Unit A

1¾"→
5½"→
1¾"→

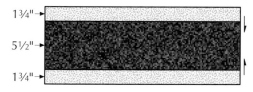

Strip Unit B

2¾"→
1½"→
1½"→
1½"→
2¾"→

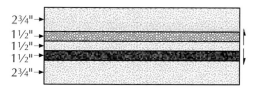

Strip Unit C

NOTE

There are two more seams in strip unit C than in A and B. If your seams are not exactly ¼" wide, the extra seams in strip unit C won't line up correctly. The finished widths of the border fabrics in strip units A and B must be exactly 5", and the finished width of the three center strips of strip unit C must be exactly 3". Double-check by laying strip unit C on strip unit A. Line up the seam of the lowest 1"-wide strip of C with the lowest seam in A as shown. Measure and mark with pins the center of A and the center of C's top 1"-wide strip. The centers must match. Repeat with strip unit B.

If your strip units don't pass these tests, fix them before proceeding.

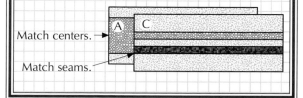

Match centers. → A C

Match seams.

2. Make 1½"-wide crosscuts.

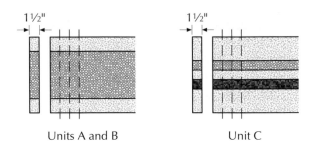

Units A and B   Unit C

3. Sew a crosscut C to crosscuts A and B, matching the seams as shown. Note the positions of the fabrics in crosscut C.

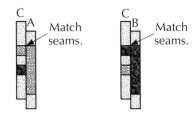

4. Sew a B/C crosscut pair to each A/C crosscut pair, matching the seams as shown.

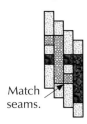

Match seams.

5. Sew the pairs into fours, and the fours into eights, maintaining the pattern and continuing until the borders are long enough for the quilt top. (See "Corners" at right.)
6. Press all seam allowances in one direction, pressing carefully to avoid distorting the bias edges.

CORNERS

The finished length of each side of the quilt top before the Twined border is added must be equal to a number of complete repeats plus an additional one-half repeat. For example:

10 repeats x 5.66" each = 56.6" + 2.83" = 59.4"
15 repeats x 5.66" each = 84.9" + 2.83" = 87.7"

Round the lengths of the borders to the nearest ⅛" or ¼", and add coping strips to bring the quilt top up to the desired measurements. (See "Making a Border That Fits" on pages 7–11.)

1. Sew each border, going from left to right, starting and ending with a C/B crosscut pair.
2. To the right end of each border, add another C/A pair and then another C/B pair. Trim, leaving a ¼"-wide seam allowance.

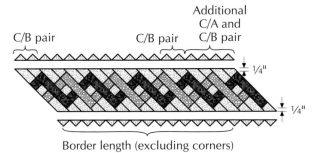

C/B pair   C/B pair   Additional C/A and C/B pair

¼"

¼"

Border length (excluding corners)

3. Cut 2 background squares, each 2⅞" x 2⅞"; cut each square in half once diagonally and sew a triangle to the right end of each border as shown.

2⅞"

Add triangle.

4. Trim the right end of each border even with the edge of the triangle.

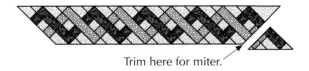

Trim here for miter.

5. Sew the borders to all 4 sides of the quilt top, starting and stopping ¼" from each corner of the quilt.
6. Miter the corners. (See "Corners" on pages 10–11.)

CHANGING THE SIZE

The directions above make a Twined border with 1"-wide finished strips. For a larger Twined border with 1½"-wide finished strips, use the cutting dimensions in the chart below and make 2"-wide crosscuts. The width of this border is 6.36", and the repeat unit is 8.48".

Strip Unit	Fabric A	Fabric B	Background
A	8"	—	2¼"
B	—	8"	2¼"
C	2"	2"	2"
			3¾"
Corner Triangles	3⅞" x 3⅞" squares, cut in half once diagonally		

VARIATIONS

The Twined border can be made from just one fabric plus the background. The intertwined illusion is lost, but it is still an interesting border design.

For another variation, substitute an additional fabric for the center background strip in strip unit C.

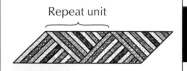

Repeat unit

Speed-Pieced Braid

Finished border width: 3.53"

Finished size of repeat unit: 7.07"

Braid borders are striking and surprisingly easy to make. This particular braid looks best if you use at least five different fabrics. Be sure to include some contrast in the fabrics. If they are all dark or all light, the braid design will be indistinct. Striped fabrics are particularly effective in braid borders; cut the fabric so the stripes run lengthwise down the strip unit.

PLANNING YOUR BORDER

Each strip unit will make about 28" of border. Estimate the amount of fabric you need from the examples below.

Quilt Size	Total Length of Borders	No. of Strip Units	Braid Fabric
Wall quilt (30" x 45")	150"	8	2⅓ yds.
Bed quilt (90" x 110")	400"	18	5 yds.

CUTTING AND ASSEMBLY

See "Speed Piecing" on pages 25–26.

1. Construct a strip unit from 10 strips, cutting each strip 1" wide. Press the seam allowances in one direction.

> **HINT HINT HINT HINT HINT HINT**
>
> *Because the strips are so narrow, the strip unit will curl uncomfortably as you sew it. To keep it flat, press each seam before proceeding to the next one. It is easiest to sew the strips together into pairs, the pairs into fours, and so on.*

> **NOTE**
>
> *The crosscuts must be squares. Measure your strip unit in several places. If it is not 5½" wide, either alter some seams, add a strip, or remove one to make the strip unit 5½" wide. Or, you can make your crosscuts the same width as the strip unit. For example, if your strip unit is 5" wide, make 5"-wide crosscuts. Be aware, however, that this will change the size of the border.*

2. Make 5½"-wide crosscuts.

5½"

3. Cut each crosscut in half once diagonally, alternating the direction of the diagonal cuts as shown.

4. Repeat steps 1–3, making the number of strip units required for your borders. For each strip unit, change the order of the fabrics. Use some fabrics in some of the strip units and omit them from others.

5. Make 2 stacks of triangles, with the triangles in one stack mirror images of the triangles in the other stack.

6. Sew together pairs of triangles, one from each stack. See the "Arrows" Hint box on page 70 to sew this seam accurately. Sew the pairs together into fours, and the fours together into eights, continuing until the borders are long enough for the quilt.

CORNERS

Each border strip must begin and end with a complete triangle. The finished length of each side of the quilt top before the Speed-Pieced Braid border is added must be equal to a number of complete triangles. For example:

10 triangles x 7.07" each = 70.7"
15 triangles x 7.07" each = 106"

Round the lengths of the borders to the nearest ⅛" or ¼", and add coping strips to bring the quilt top up to the desired measurements. (See "Making a Border That Fits" on pages 7–11.)

Be careful not to flip any of the borders; keep them identical, with the strips of the inner triangles oriented in the same direction as shown.

1. Sew together enough triangles to fit each side of the quilt top.

2. Add 1 more triangle to each end of each border strip. (See diagram above right.)

3. Sew the borders to the 4 sides of the quilt top, starting and stopping ¼" from the corners.

4. Miter the corners. (See "Corners" on pages 10–11.)

CHANGING THE SIZE

The strip unit can be any width. The repeat unit is always 1.41 times the finished width of the strip unit; that is, the total width of the strip unit minus ½". The width of the border is half the repeat unit. Since the strip units go into squares, the width of each border is the same as the total width of the strip unit. Here are some examples:

Finished Width of Strip Unit	Repeat Unit	Width of Border
3"	4.24"	2.12"
7½"	10.58"	5.29"
10"	14.10"	7.05"

VARIATIONS

For a more restrained braid border, use fewer fabrics and make all the strip units identical.

For a less restrained braid border, cut the strips in a variety of widths. This is a particularly good idea if you have trouble making your strip units the required width—or getting them all to turn out the same width. Just keep adding strips until you have the correct width, trimming the strip unit a bit if you overshoot.

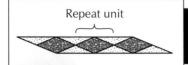

Repeat unit

Diamonds

Finished border width: 1.40"

Finished size of repeat unit: 3.24"

This is a slim, elegant speed-pieced border.

PLANNING YOUR BORDER

Each strip unit will make about 52" of border. Estimate the amount of fabric you need from the examples below.

Quilt Size	Total Length of Borders	No. of Strip Units	Diamond Fabric	Background Fabric
Wall quilt (30" x 45")	150"	3	¼ yd.	½ yd.
Bed quilt (90" x 110")	400"	8	½ yd.	1¼ yds.

CUTTING AND ASSEMBLY

See "Speed Piecing" on pages 25–26.

1. Construct a strip unit, cutting the strips the widths shown in the diagram. Stagger each strip 1½" from the end of the last strip. Press the seam allowances as indicated.

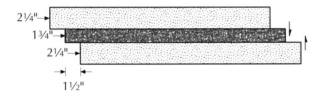

2¼"
1¾"
2¼"
1½"

2. Trim one end of the strip unit at a 45° angle. Make 1¾"-wide crosscuts, maintaining the 45° angle.

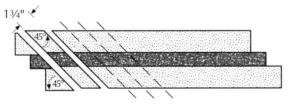

1¾"
45°
45°

3. Join crosscuts in pairs, matching the seams as shown.

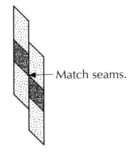

Match seams.

4. Sew the pairs into fours, and the fours into eights, continuing until the borders are long enough for the quilt top. Press the seam allowances in one direction, pressing carefully to avoid distorting the bias edges.

5. Trim the long edges, leaving a ¼"-wide seam allowance.

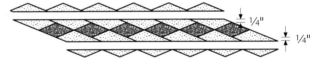

¼"
¼"

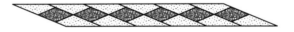

CORNERS

Two possible corners are shown. For the first, each border strip begins and ends with a whole diamond. The finished length of each side of the quilt top before adding the Diamonds border must be equal to a number of complete diamonds. For example:

10 diamonds x 3.26" each = 32.6"
22 diamonds x 3.26" each = 71.2"

Round the lengths of the borders to the nearest ⅛" or ¼", and add coping strips to bring the quilt top up to the desired measurements. (See "Making a Border That Fits" on pages 7–11.)

1. Add a 1¾"-wide background strip to each end of the border. Trim the edges and the ends as shown. Sew the top and bottom borders to the quilt top.

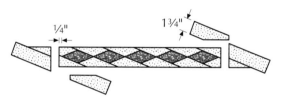

2. Cut and add 2" corner squares of background fabric to each end of the side borders.

3. Sew the side borders to the quilt top, then trim the edges of the corners even with the ends of the borders.

For the second corner variation, plan the borders so the diamond tips touch at the corners. The length of each side of the quilt top before the Diamonds border is added must be equal to a number of complete diamonds plus one-half of a diamond. For example:

10 diamonds x 3.26" each = 32.6" + 1.63" = 34.2"
22 diamonds x 3.26" each = 71.72" + 1.63" = 73.4"

Round the lengths of the borders to the nearest ⅛" or ¼", and add coping strips to bring the quilt top up to the desired measurements. (See "Making a Border That Fits" on pages 7–11.)

1. For each border strip, round the number of diamonds up. For example, if the side of the quilt top is 10½ diamonds long, make the border from 11 diamonds. One-fourth of a diamond length will overhang the end of each border.

2. Add a 1¾"-wide background strip to each end of the borders. Trim the long edges, but *do not trim the ends yet.*

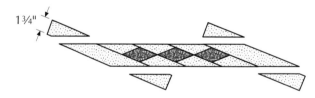

3. Sew each border strip to the quilt top, starting and stopping ¼" from the edges of the quilt top. (The borders will extend beyond the corners of the quilt top.) Miter the corners, matching the points of the diamonds at the end of each border strip. (See "Corners" on pages 10–11.)

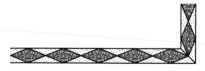

4. After sewing the miter seam, trim the seam allowance to ¼". Trim the corners, using the long edges of the borders as a guide.

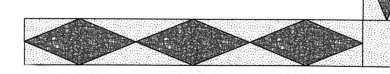

CHANGING THE SIZE

To make borders with larger diamonds, follow the chart below for the dimensions to cut and stagger the strips in the strip unit. The directions on the previous page are for a border 1.40" wide.

Border Width	Repeat Unit	Diamond Strip Width	Background Strip Width	Stagger Each	Crosscut Width
1.12"	2.60"	1½"	2"	1¼"	1½"
1.40"	3.24"	1¾"	2¼"	1½"	1¾"
1.68"	3.88"	2"	2½"	1¾"	2"
1.96"	4.54"	2¼"	2¾"	2"	2¼"
2.23"	5.20"	2½"	3"	2¼"	2½"

VARIATIONS

For a scrappy border, make shorter strip units using many fabrics, then arrange the crosscuts randomly. You could also use two or three fabrics and arrange the diamonds in a repeating design.

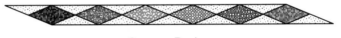

Scrappy Design

Repeating Design

Accordion Pleats

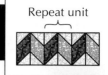

Finished border width: 3.62"

Finished size of repeat unit: 3"

Choose your fabrics carefully for this border. Select one fabric a little darker than the other to create the illusion of an accordion-folded border.

PLANNING YOUR BORDER

Each set of strip units will make about 42" of border. Estimate the amount of fabric you need from the examples below.

Quilt Size	Total Length of Borders	No. of Strip Unit Sets	A and B Fabric	Background Fabric
Wall quilt (30" x 45")	150"	4	⅓ yd. each	¾ yd.
Bed quilt (90" x 110")	400"	10	⅔ yd. each	1¾ yds.

CUTTING AND ASSEMBLY

See "Speed Piecing" on pages 25–26.

1. Construct strip units A and B, cutting the strips the widths shown in the diagram. Stagger the left end of each strip 1" from the previous strip, and make strip units A and B mirror images of each other. Press the seam allowances as shown.

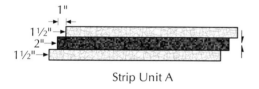

Strip Unit A

Strip Unit B

2. Trim the left end of each strip unit at a 45° angle.

3. From each strip unit, make 2"-wide cross-cuts parallel to the 45° angle to get mirror images.

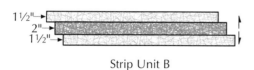

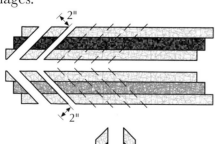

A   B

4. Join 1 crosscut from each strip unit into pairs, matching the seams.

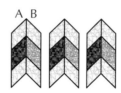

A B

5. Sew the pairs into fours, and the fours into eights, continuing until the borders are long enough for the quilt top. Press the seam allowances in one direction, pressing carefully to avoid distorting the bias edges.

6. Trim the long edges, leaving a ¼"-wide seam allowance.

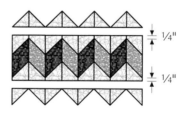

¼"

¼"

CORNERS

Each border must begin with a crosscut A and end with a crosscut B. The finished length of each side of the quilt top before the Accordion-Pleat border is added must be equal to a number of complete repeats plus one-half of a repeat. For example:

10 repeats x 3.62" each = 36.2" + 1.86" = 38.1"
22 repeats x 3.62" each = 79.6" + 1.86" = 81.5"

Round the lengths of the borders to the nearest ⅛" or ¼", and add coping strips to bring the quilt top up to the desired measurements. (See "Making a Border That Fits" on pages 7–11.)

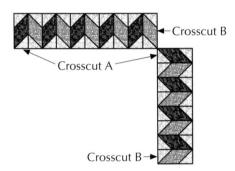

Crosscut B
Crosscut A
Crosscut B

1. Each corner square requires a pair of crosscuts, one from strip unit A and one from strip unit B. Remove the bottom background triangle from each crosscut. Sew the 2 crosscuts together as shown; stop stitching ¼" from the inside corner for the inset seam in step 2. Press seams open.

Discard.

Stop stitching here.

2. Cut a 3" square of background fabric and inset it as shown. (See Hint box below.) Trim the excess fabric.

HINT HINT HINT HINT HINT HINT

To sew the inset seam, pin and sew from A to B, backstitching at both ends. Repin and sew from A to C, backstitching at both ends.

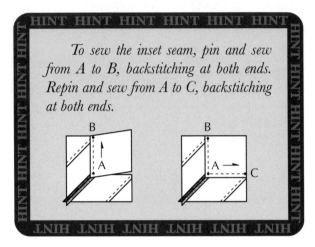

3. Sew the side borders to the quilt top. Sew a corner unit to each end of the top and bottom borders, then sew to the quilt top.

CHANGING THE SIZE

To make a smaller or larger border design, cut the strips in the following widths.

Border Width	Repeat Unit Width	A and B Strip	Background Strip	Crosscut Width
2.41"	2"	1½"	1¼"	1½"
4.82"	4"	2½"	2"	2½"

VARIATIONS

Make taller accordion pleats by cutting the crosscuts narrower than the cut width of the fabric A and B strips. Use squares of background fabric for the corner squares.

You can make a Double Accordion Pleats border by including two shades of fabric A in strip unit A, and two shades of fabric B in strip unit B. The corner blocks are constructed in much the same way as the single Accordion Pleats border, but use four crosscuts instead of two.

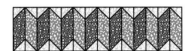

For another look, edge the strips of fabrics A and B with narrow strips of two shades of accent fabrics.

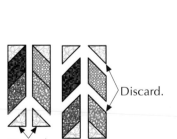

Discard.

Discard.

Add square and sides.

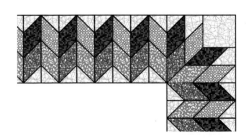

FOUNDATION - PIECING PATTERNS

Use the patterns on these pages for making miniature versions of some of the borders in this book.
For foundation-piecing instructions, see pages 26–27. For information about corners and ideas about fabric
selection, see the directions for each border. If you do not find the exact size of your quilt in this section,
photocopy the patterns, enlarging or reducing them to fit your quilt.

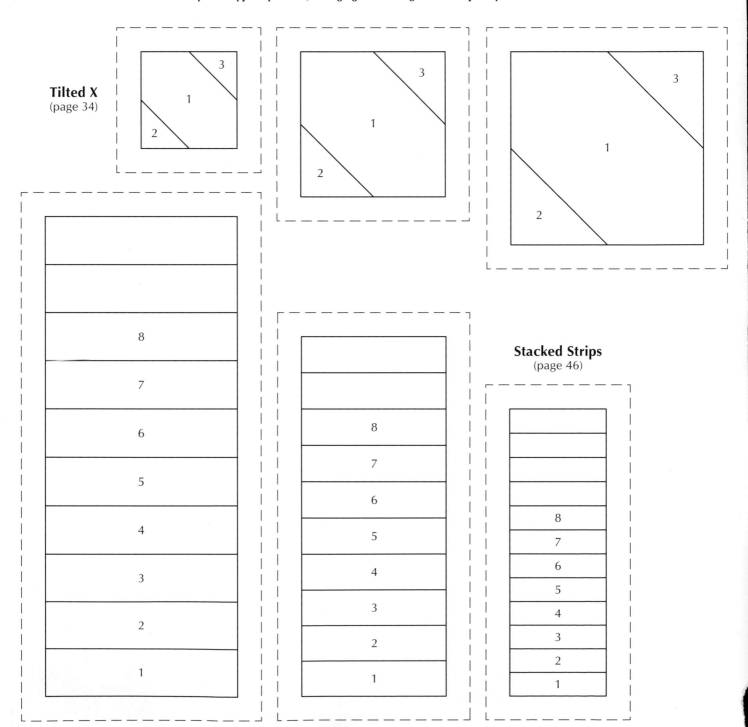

Tilted X
(page 34)

Stacked Strips
(page 46)

Easy Braid
(page 28)

Log Cabin Spiral
(page 30)

Small Dogtooth
(page 60)

Flying Geese
(page 32)

Eeek! Mice!
(page 38)

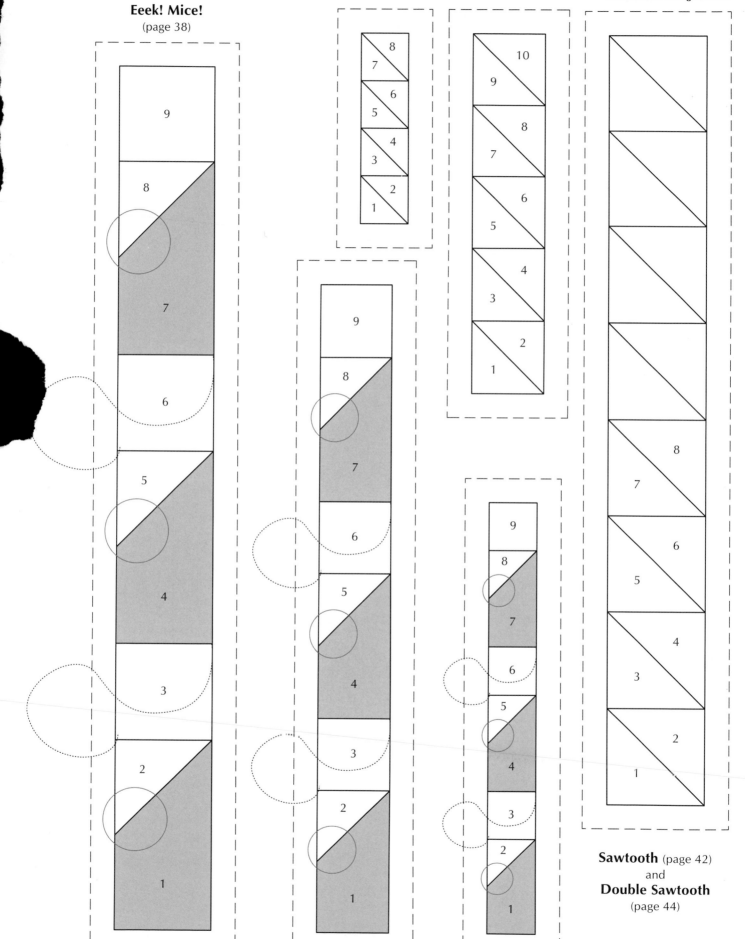

Sawtooth (page 42)
and
Double Sawtooth
(page 44)

Arrows
(page 69)

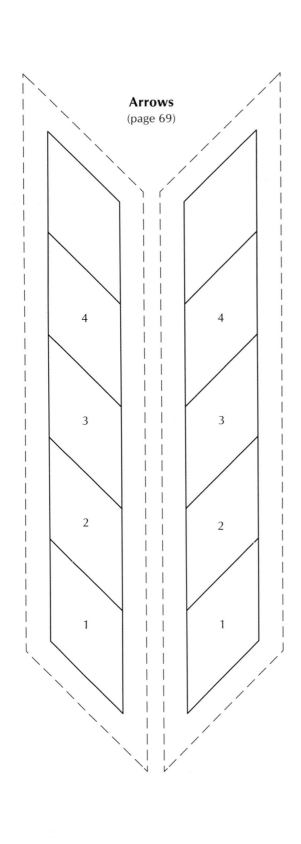

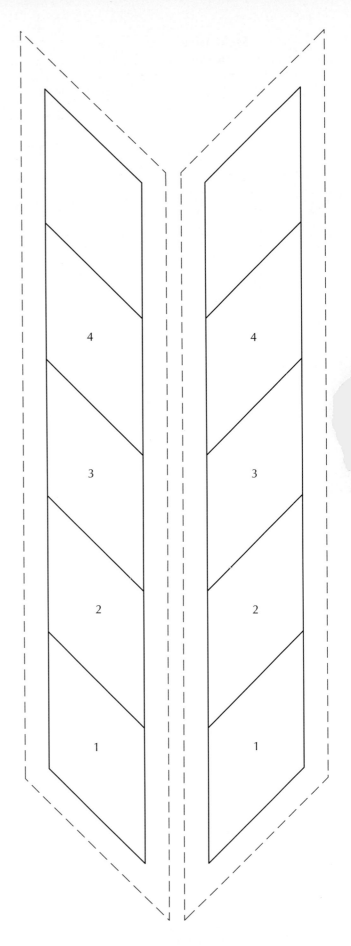

ABOUT THE AUTHOR

Janet Kime teaches and lectures about quiltmaking throughout the Pacific Northwest and edits the newsletter for her local quilt guild, Needle and I. This is her fourth book with That Patchwork Place. In addition to her busy schedule of quilting activities, Janet is employed full-time as an academic counselor and publications coordinator at the University of Washington in Seattle. She and her goats and cats live on rural Vashon Island.

Publications and Products

Many titles are available at your local quilt shop.
For more information, write for a free color catalog
to That Patchwork Place, Inc., PO Box 118, Bothell,
WA 98041-0118 USA.

☎ U.S. and Canada, call **1-800-426-3126** for the
name and location of the quilt shop nearest you.
Int'l: 1-425-483-3313   **Fax:** 1-425-486-7596
E-mail: info@patchwork.com
Web: www.patchwork.com   7.97